THE
GREAT
FAILURE

THE
GREAT
FAILURE

A Bartender, a Monk,
and My Unlikely Path to Truth

NATALIE
GOLDBERG

HarperSanFrancisco
A Division of HarperCollins*Publishers*

Dogen poem from *The Sea and the Honeycomb: A Book of Tiny Poems,* ed. by Robert Bly © 1971 by Robert Bly. Reprinted by permission of Robert Bly.

Excerpt from "Case 13: Te-shan: Bowls in Hand" *The Gateless Barrier* translated by Robert Aitken. Copyright © 1991 by Diamond Sangha. Reprinted by permission of North Point Press, a division of Farrar, Straus and Giroux, LLC.

A small portion of this book was published in *Shambhala Sun,* July 2002.

HarperCollins books may be purchased for educational, business, or sales promotional use. For information please write: Special Markets Department, HarperCollins Publishers, Inc., 10 East 53rd Street, New York, NY 10022.

HarperCollins Web site: http://www.harpercollins.com

HarperCollins®, 📖 ®, and HarperSanFrancisco™ are trademarks of HarperCollins Publishers, Inc.

FIRST EDITION

Library of Congress Cataloging-in-Publication Data is available upon request.
ISBN 0–06–073399–3

04 05 06 07 08 RRD(H) 10 9 8 7 6 5 4 3 2 1

For Michèle

Acknowledgments

THANK YOU TO Erik Storlie, Tamara Kaiser, Rob Wilder, Eddie Lewis, Wendy Johnson, Judith Ragir, Jisho Warner, Jean Leyshon, and Liz Visick. Also to Dunn Brothers in Minneapolis, Bread and Chocolate in St. Paul, Minnesota, the Four Arts Society Library in Palm Beach, Florida, the Menlo Park Public Library, and the Prolific Oven Bakery in Palo Alto, California, where I wrote much of this.

The following books were very helpful: *Zen's Chinese Heritage* by Andrew Ferguson (Wisdom Publications, 2000), *Book of Serenity,* translated by Thomas Cleary (Shambhala, 1988), and *The Blue Cliff Record,* translated by Thomas Cleary and J. C. Cleary.

Geri Thoma, my agent, Gideon Weil, my editor—I appreciate you.

THE
GREAT
FAILURE

Introduction

She knows there's no success like failure,
And that failure's no success at all.

— BOB DYLAN

AFTER MY ZEN TEACHER DIED, a fellow practitioner said to me, "Natalie, your writing succeeded. You didn't follow the teachings. Everything Roshi taught us was about how to fail."

We both laughed.

But I think it was true that we were trained in defeat. Downfall brings us to the ground, facing the nitty-gritty, things as they are with no glitter. Success cannot last forever. Everyone's time runs out. This is not a popular notion, but it is true.

Achievement solidifies us. Believing we are invincible, we want more and more. It makes us hungry. But we can be caught in the opposite too. Human beings manage to also drown in the pool of despair, seeped in the mud of depression. We spend our life on a roller coaster with rusty tracks, stuck to highs and lows, riding from one, trying to grab the other.

To heal ourselves from this painful cycle—the severe split we create and then the quasi equilibrium we try to maintain—we have to crash. Only then can we drop through to a more authentic self.

Zen transmits its legacy from this deeper place. It is a different kind of failure: the Great Failure, a boundless surrender. Nothing to hold on to and nothing to lose. Sitting still, feeling our breath, we watch the electric animals of desire and aggression arise and pass away. Our arms spread wide, we welcome it all. In the Great Failure we find the Great Success. They are no longer different from one another. Both dissolve into the moment. Illusions break open and we can be real with ourselves and the people around us. When obstructions are swept away, we can see clearly. Here we are, with our lives in our hands. Who were we? Who are we?

I write about my two fathers, my natural one and my spiritual one. Each was a powerful man. I loved them both. I tell incidents that happened, matters not often talked about. I am looking down the raw throat of their lives. In doing this I am also facing my own. How I was deceived, disregarded, offended, how I was naïve, ignorant, foolish—the things no one wants to behold.

Why am I doing this? Because it is a way to liberation, bringing us into intimate connection with human life. And what is the best approach? Of course, the hardest and most obvious: through the people we are close to. Not through some flashy movie star on the screen, but in contact with our wrinkles, our scars, with the sad way a father missed his chance in love, as though he thought time would last forever.

The Great Failure is a boundless embrace, leaving nothing out. We hear the words "repression," "denial," "rationalization," any method to squirm away. But in the end this kind of coping only leads to more pain. Entire wars have been based on our inability to see.

I wanted to learn the truth, to become whole. If I could touch the dark nature in someone else, I could know it in myself. I wrote this book in the hope of meeting what's real. It is my humble effort to illuminate the path of honesty.

PART 1

Don't worry if you write the truth. It doesn't hurt people, it helps them.

—Dainin Katagiri Roshi

WITH ORANGE LEAVES STILL CLINGING to branches in that unusually mild stretch of late fall, on a sweet street in quiet St. Paul, I was about to slip my key into the front door of the apartment building. I was returning from Zen Center, where I came to study for two months. It was Monday at nine in the evening; no one was on the street. Suddenly I jerked my head to the right. One step below me in the entryway stood a beautiful man, shining face, almost clear eyes, in his late teens, aiming the barrel of a shotgun right at my neck. Feeling the small opening circle on my skin, I jerked my head.

"How dare you!" I was about to be outraged when he hissed, "Don't make a move. Give me your purse."

On my left shoulder dangled a small black backpack with three hundred dollars in twenty-dollar bills. Just that day I had been to the bank. To my chest I clutched my spiral notebook, the hefty 463-page *Book of Serenity* containing one hundred Zen dialogues, and a thinner black paperback, *Transmission of Light*.

On my right shoulder was a big blue plastic bag advertising a pharmaceutical company in white letters. My friend, a dermatologist, had picked it up for me at a medical convention. This bag held my old brown sneakers,

black pants I bought when I returned a gift sweater that
was too small, a Bob Dylan T-shirt a student had given me
fifteen years ago, and a pair of good socks. I had gone to
the gym only three times in the last month. That afternoon was my third time.

"C'mon, give it up."

I looked at him. He was nervous. Was this his first?
Or was he on drugs? In a magnanimous moment I
handed over my exercise bag.

"This is your purse?" He took a step back and sur-
veyed me.

"Yes," I said emphatically.

"You sure?" I nodded my head up and down in
earnest. We were having a fashion disagreement.

He turned and ran. I bolted through the front door. I
had fooled him. He could keep those worn gym shoes. I
felt a small victory.

FIVE DAYS LATER I was standing on the podium during a
conference at a Marriott Hotel in Fort Lauderdale,
Florida. Seven hundred people were staring up at me.
The title of my talk was "Riding Your Wild Horses." I
was supposed to be speaking about creative writing, but
the night before I had decided to change the whole lecture. In St. Paul I'd been studying Zen koans, short inter-
changes between teachers and students from eighth- and
ninth-century China that cut through conditioned ways
of seeing, enabling a person to experience one's true

nature. I wanted to talk about that in my keynote speech, then to link it up to my being robbed, another kind of wake-up experience. I was sure it would work. I loved giving talks. Eventually, I'd meander over and tie it up with writing to fulfill the obligation of my original contract. This felt adventuresome and I was pleased. I made three notes on the smallest torn-off corner of a piece of paper and went to bed.

A tall lovely man who had read my books introduced me. I stepped onto the stage and thanked him. I took a sip of water and began by telling an ancient teaching tale.

Te-shan, a learned Buddhist scholar, piled up all his sutras—they weighed a lot—put them in a bag on his back, and headed south. Te-shan thought the Zen practitioners in southern China who espoused direct insight not dependent on book learning had it all wrong, and he was going to set them straight. On the way—of course he walked, maybe for a portion of the journey taking a boat down the Yangtze—he met an old woman selling tea cakes on the side of the road. He stopped for some refreshment. But the old woman, instead of setting out the provisions, inquired, "What's on your back?"

"They are commentaries and teachings of the Buddha."

"They are indeed! Well, if you're so learned, may I ask you a question? If you can answer it, the food is free, but if you fail, you get nothing."

Our Te-shan with all his book learning thought this would be simple, like taking candy from a babe. He agreed.

The woman then asked—and with her question I could feel my audience fading, that vital link between speaker and listener suddenly going limp—"If the mind does not exist in the past, and the present mind does not exist, and there's also no mind in the future, tell me with what mind will you receive these cakes?"

What is she talking about? Before the old woman's question, the audience was willing to come along. After all, everyone loves a story, and certainly Natalie Goldberg was leading up to those wild horses advertised in the catalog. Maybe the old woman will even pull them out of her cakes. Oh, the audience was hopeful. I could feel it. This was a conference full of crystals, psychics, healing dances, drums, auras, afterlives.

The question stunned Te-shan. He could not fathom an answer. Speechless, he wasn't even a match for a roadside cake seller, no less an ordinary woman. He knew he had to abandon his bold decision to challenge the southern teachers of Zen. All his scholarly learning had led to nothing. No lunch for him.

Now, it was here in my talk that I planned to swoop down and point out that these unnamed old women in koans appear to have great wisdom, but they happen to be... what was I talking about anyway? Where did I think this was going to lead? Was I attempting to compare the old woman with my robber? The old woman had blown Te-shan's mind. My mind had been blown too, but it was only five days after I was accosted—it was too soon for me to make any sense of it. Besides, this audience did not have to witness my struggle for personal realization. What was I doing standing up in front of everyone anyway? I wanted my stolen brown shoes and my Dylan shirt back. Every face in the audience was suddenly the same—the face of my thief. They had signed up for this lovely New Age weekend down in Florida—what was going on with this Natalie Goldberg? I knew only a handful had read any of my books. How was I going to leap over this mess smoothly and talk about writing practice, where I was on solid ground? I mentioned the horses from the title—ahh, relief on their faces—they had come to the correct lecture hall after all.

Then everything dropped away. I had nothing to say. I glanced at my little white piece of paper. No help there. I looked at my wristwatch. I was supposed to be up there for a full hour. Forty-five more minutes to go. I was being paid big bucks for this talk.

Total silence. Into a long pause I asked, "Would you like to hear a poem?"

Everyone nodded, relieved.

I knew one poem by heart. "It's by Dogen, a thirteenth-century Zen master."

Nobody's face registered any recognition. I plunged ahead anyway:

> *This slowly drifting cloud is pitiful;*
> *What dreamwalkers men become.*

Awakened, I hear the one true thing—
Black rain on the roof of Fukakusa temple.

It went over like a dead—not a wild—horse.

"Would you like to hear it again?" Of course, they wouldn't, but I dove in and recited it even more dramatically a second time. Then I asked the dumbest question. "How many of you liked it?" I already knew the answer. Eight people out of seven hundred raised their hands.

People in the back of the room were getting up and leaving. "Well, does anyone have a question?" I asked brightly.

Immediately ushers rushed into the aisles with mikes. The organizers must have felt relief—she's doing something. Questioners formed small lines, awaiting their chance to speak.

A man's amplified voice: "How do you know if you're writing something good? I mean, you could be working on something for six months, and it could be shit."

Now here was my medium. There was no angle of writing for which I couldn't come up with a helpful answer. But instead of launching into my authoritative voice, I just stood there and quietly said, "I don't know. It's up to each one of us to find our own way."

He nodded seriously.

A frail young woman in sandals and a gray and white checkered shift stepped to the mike. "I want to write this story. It's partly true, about my brother, but I'm afraid he'll kill me if he reads it."

This is an old question about privacy. I'd answered it many times and been, I think, helpful.

Instead, I cocked my head and just kept looking at this woman. I noticed, but without thinking about it, more like the way a clay plate registers the placement on its surface of a carrot, a radish and a slice of cucumber— open and indifferent—that she wore small turquoise earrings, one gold bangle on her right wrist, had a long thin scar from her left ankle up to right below her shinbone. I understood right then that I couldn't help anyone.

It came to mind that she wanted an answer to her question. "You have to make your own decision." I meant it with all my heart—but not particularly to that specific inquiry.

A few more people fumbled up to the mike, while most of the audience dashed for the exits. I glanced at my watch. "Only five minutes left," I said cheerily. "One more person."

"What's it like to be a famous writer?"

Now things were getting loopy. I smiled so my substantial teeth and pink gums showed. I gave a little bow—the Buddhist way, with hands together in front of me—and then I slithered off the stage. Please no one ever see me again. Should I go to the officials and tell them to keep their big check? I'd never goofed like this. Maybe I was just imagining how bad I was. Then I remembered the old tea-cake woman's question and winced. Yeah, I was terrible. No one wanted to hear this stuff, especially from me. I didn't know what I was talking about.

I left the building looking straight ahead, glancing neither right nor left. I made it to my rented Hyundai and barreled out of the parking lot, heading north to the small seaside town of Lake Worth.

The plan was to visit my parents after the conference. They lived ten miles inland in a senior community called Buttonwood, where squat, unattached units lined up behind well-trimmed lawns. Bougainvillea, palms, and wandering jews edged along the front walks. Houseplants that were put out one day while the cleaning person mopped were forgotten and grew into towering trees.

Though I had made good time, my parents were waiting for me eagerly as though I were late.

"Was there traffic? Here, sit." My father scooped chicken onto his plate. "Get your own, Nat." This was business. Take your fill and eat.

My mother rushed back and forth, to the stove for sweet potatoes, then to the refrigerator for applesauce. "You want water? It's cold. I took it from the tap and put it in the freezer just before you came." She reached in for an old brown prune-juice jar now full of water.

"Any Perrier?" I asked.

My father raised his left eyebrow—both are substantial, thick, silver, bushy, above piercing blue eyes. "That stuff is toilet water. They bottle it, and then the fools hand over their good dollar bills. What a racket."

"So, Nat, how did your talk go?" my mother asked with her mouth full of lettuce. This question was unusual. When I visited them, my individual life dropped away. Never was there a mention of my life beyond the arms of the family. I was fifty years old. It made no difference. My father's only comment on the phone when I told him at thirty-five that I was getting a divorce was, "So now will you move back home?"

But why this time would my mother ask, this single time when I'd failed miserably?

I ignored the question. This usually is a good tactic. I commented on the meal. The interest in food would sweep any conversation under.

A moment later she actually asked again. "Tell us about your talk." Not only that, but my father stopped eating, poultry leg dangling halfway to his mouth, grease around his lips. He too wanted to hear how it went.

"Oh, really good." That should have been enough.

But it wasn't. "How many people were there?" my mother wanted to know.

"This kasha is really good. I like the onions."

"How many?" My father put down the leg.

"Seven hundred."

"What did you tell them?" No one but me was eating now.

"Oh, a Zen story—a koan—and then I brought it over to writing." Of course, I never mentioned the mugging. At all costs protect your parents.

"What's a koan?" I was backed into a corner. They were paying attention.

"A teaching story."

"Well, c'mon, Nat. Tell it to us. You know, like we were the audience. Talk."

By now I had become as pale as the turnip on my plate. I took a deep breath. "Well, Te-shan is a learned man who lives in northern China . . ."

They were listening intently. I could feel their raw attention, as palpable as a small animal in my hand. All at once I was transmitting the dharma in my parents' Florida kitchen. My head was whirling. If these teachings were able to reach my father's ears—I glanced over at his big floppy lobes—then Zen could truly take root in this country.

I encouraged myself: keep going, Nat. I got to the old woman. My mother's eyes narrowed. "What kind of cakes?" she asked.

I made it up. "Honey cakes with poppy seeds."

"Mmm, must have been good. That man was hungry," my mother said. "It was a long trip."

"So what's the question the old woman's gonna ask?" My father was impatient. He was a gambler. He wanted to see if Te-shan could win the cake.

"Okay." I spoke in a gruff storytelling whisper. This

time I was going to make the story work. "She holds a morsel in front of his nose. She speaks, 'If present mind does not exist, if past mind does not exist'"—with these few utterances from the ancient woman again I've lost my audience. That warm furry animal I held in the palm of my hand dashed out. I clenched an empty fist.

My father crinkled his nose as if something near him stunk. Once more I smelled the dead horse. My mother stuck out her tongue.

My father's nostrils quivered. "They paid you all that money for that?"

I nodded, my lips pressed together in a tight rib of agreement. I commiserated with him. Life just doesn't make sense.

I've been through all this before. I never learn. The time before was at the beginning of a weeklong visit. My father and I went to the Gourmet Deli for lunch. We hadn't seen each other in eight months. Things felt fresh, and we were both hungry. I ordered a corned beef sandwich. He wanted two big specials, large beefy hot dogs with plenty of sauerkraut and mustard, and fries. He ordered an IBC root beer. Recently he had found this beverage in a store and acted as though he had discovered America. "Nat, these are the greatest. You should have one." Then he scrunched his face. "Naa, forget it. They're expensive. Stay with the free water." My father must have really loved them. Usually he wouldn't have spent extra money.

After the waitress took our order and left, we sat cheered in anticipation of a good meal and a week together. In a madras shirt, material taut, the two buttons over his middle strained, the plaid zigzagging, his thick-fisted hands clenched together in front of him, my father tried to think what next to say to his educated daughter. He had owned a tough bar on Long Island for thirty years and day after day watched those from the seedier side of life drink themselves under. He had risen with his own tough nature to meet their pain and make his living. But now he suddenly had a question, and he asked it enthusiastically—life at that moment seemed full of possibility. "Nat, so tell me—what is Buddhism anyway? They talk about it on TV. I even read about it in *Time* magazine. I don't get it. Explain it to me."

I'd spent hundreds of hours doing zazen, back straight, legs crossed, feeling my breath go in and out, and now here was my chance. My father wanted to know what I surely must understand.

I chose my words carefully and tried to keep it simple and direct. "Well, Dad, it's about being present, moment by moment. So when you're drinking a glass of water, you just drink a glass of water. When you walk, you walk—"

My father's eyes bugged out of his head, and he leaned in over the table. "You've got to be kidding," he interrupted me. "That's ridiculous."

My head jerked back: he's right. What had I been

thinking? Why couldn't I have followed his example? His mind always stayed dead ahead of him. His life was congruent. One thing followed another. Nothing in the way. He went to war, he came home, he married, he worked, he had children, he grew old and retired to Florida. What was the problem? What else was there? Sure, once in a while he wondered about his dead mother, Rose, or what it would have been like to have had a son, but these were only brief musings. My father's life was the horse in front of him. He got on it and rode.

Then for a moment he softened. He put his big paw over mine, "Nat . . ." But he never finished the sentence. The waitress had come and laid those plates of juicy meat in front of us. Words dropped. We dug in.

THE VERY FIRST TIME my parents challenged my zen life happened in New Mexico, that land of coyotes, sage, dirt roads, woodstoves—absurd things, but because their daughter was there, Ben and Syl Goldberg schlepped out.

They are visiting me in my new home in Santa Fe. Already they have let me know I've gotten a bad deal on the house. I paid much too much. Now in the cool late July afternoon we are sitting on the porch. Amazingly, we're not eating. We are sitting in a line. I am in the middle.

"Hey, Nat," my father begins, "what is meditation?"

"It's hard to explain." Then because I am still incredibly foolish, I have a brilliant, daring idea. "Do you want to try?" And before they can answer I run into the house and get a bell.

Accoutrements, I think, will make it official.

"Okay, when I ring the bell you just sit and feel your breath go in and out at your nose. If your mind wanders, just bring it back gently to your breath. We'll sit for ten minutes."

"Okay," they both say, suddenly eager—this will be fun—and they wriggle in their chairs to compose themselves.

The bell sounds three times, and we settle into this most ordinary thing—people breathing next to each other. My father is on my right, my mother on my left. I cannot believe this is happening. Here we are, all paying attention. The ten minutes feel spacious, luscious, and forever. The shade is cool. We're all quiet. This must be what heaven is.

The time is up. I ring the bell once to mark the end of meditation.

"Well, how was it?" I ask. "Did you have a lot of distractions?"

My father shrugs his shoulders. "What's the big deal?"

"Well, did you discover how much you think? Was it hard to concentrate?"

"No, I didn't have a single thought."

"None?" I ask surprised.

"Not a one."

"Well, did you feel peaceful?"

"Not particularly. It was like how it always is when you don't talk. That's why human beings talk. Nothing is happening otherwise."

I turn to my mother. "I was aggravated the whole time about your friend. She must think I'm awful."

The night before, my mother had blurted out at dinner that she thought the chapters of my novel were awful, and my friend Frances, who was there, told me later that my mother was jealous.

I had confronted my mother that morning, and she apologized profusely. "I don't know what came over me. Your chapters are lovely."

"Let's try again," my mother says. "This time I'll do it right."

I start to explain there's no right or wrong, but instead just say, "Okay."

"This time I want to ring the bell," my father says, grabbing the stick. He ceremoniously hits the bell three times.

We are sitting for two and a half minutes when my father suddenly belts out, "Hello, Dolly. Well, hello, Dolly. It's so nice to have you back where you belong," while ringing the bell continuously to accompany himself.

"Buddy, please," my mother tries to stop him, struggling to reach across me to grab the bell, but my father keeps going. He's having a ball.

I'm the only one staring straight ahead at the high adobe wall a hundred feet in front of us, still attempting to notice my breath.

I decide right then that I don't have to save my parents. They don't count as sentient beings. They are in another category entirely.

I imagine the Enlightened One's talk under the bodhi tree. "There are ten kinds of beings"—and now Buddha turns his head and addresses me personally—"and, Natalie, your father is the eleventh kind—out of this universe."

THREE STRIKES AND YOU'RE OUT. The Te-shan story was my final dharma defeat with my parents. They were victorious forever. I had a terrible headache as I sat in their kitchen.

"This has been a long day," I said, excusing myself.

My parents gazed over across the table at me with the grace and assurance of great Thoroughbreds striding way ahead of the loser.

My father nodded his large head. "I'll meet you early tomorrow morning."

I didn't stay with them anymore—for the past ten years I'd stayed at a pink hotel on the beach, "Florida the way it used to be," the last small place in a towering strip of deluxe condominiums.

I said good night and drove alone through the dark to my hotel.

I didn't use the air conditioner, and at six in the morning I could hear my father calling out my name, "Nat, Naat," through the open screened window.

I dashed to the door in my nightgown and beckoned him to number twenty-four. "Dad, you're early. It's still dark out." He slept little at night now, dozing off intermittently in his blue TV chair.

Five months ago he had had surgery for colon cancer. When he came out of the anesthetic he bit the nurse, who was trying to prick his arm. "You've got all the blood you're gonna get out of me."

The staff couldn't wait to get rid of him. They wanted to send him to rehab right away, but he wouldn't go. He declared loudly to me on the phone, while my sister and mother sat opposite him in the hospital room, "I love you, Natalie. I love my wife. I love Romi. But so help me, if your mother doesn't take me home, I'll leave all of you. I know my body better than anyone else. I don't care what they say. I want to go home." This was his last great fight after World War II—all those enemies in the white sanitary building trying to murder him.

I looked at my father in the early morning light. His skin was yellow, and he was too thin. All at once my father had become an old man. His strong swimmer legs were like bowed sticks in his blue Bermuda shorts and sockless loafers. He had already outlived the rest of his family by twenty years. All the other Goldbergs died in their early sixties.

"Wait for me by those deck chairs." I pointed. "Watch the sun rise over the ocean. I have to do my half hour of walking."

"Okay," he easily agreed. This was enjoyable for him. Something to do, a place to be. He'd been retired for over twenty years, and life had become boring.

Before the operation, we drove to consultations with different oncologists. I wanted my father to have the best care. I didn't like the first one we visited. He was too abrupt, too sure of himself.

As we sat in the waiting room for a second opinion, my father asked where Michèle was. She had been my partner for the last five years, and we had recently moved in together. She often came down to Florida with me to visit my parents, and my mother and father had grown fond of her.

"It was hard for her yesterday, seeing all these cancer doctors. It brought up feelings about her dad."

"Didn't he die ten years ago?"

"Yes."

"So what's the problem?"

"It reminded her of how it was when he was sick."

"But it was ten years ago."

"Dad, a person can still have feelings."

"I don't understand. It was years ago. Why didn't she come?"

I rolled my eyes. "Never mind."

This doctor we liked. He complimented my father on the Hawaiian shirt he was wearing.

"My daughter gave it to me."

When he walked out of the room for a moment, my father said, "Well, at least he admires my clothes."

What other criteria did we really have? The first doctor didn't even physically examine him. This one did.

"Thank you," my father said when we were back in the car. He added no qualifier. He was genuinely appreciative. He didn't like the first physician either, but felt too helpless to stick up for himself.

In the distance at the end of the pier fishing boats were gathering bait.

"How was it?" I was sweating in my white shorts and sneakers after my walk.

My father turned up his nose. "No big deal. It was the sunrise. Let's go eat."

Even for the short distance to the restaurant he turned on the car air conditioner full blast. He put his big right hand over mine. I looked at his ruby ring, the one his mother gave him on his twentieth birthday. He'd never taken it off. One of the two small diamonds was missing, and all edges of the red gem had been rubbed smooth by wear. Once swimming in the Indian Ocean while stationed in India during the war, he came up, breaking the water's surface, and saw it was missing. With no hesitation he dove under again and grabbed two handfuls of sand. When he opened his fingers and the saltwater rushed through, the ring was in his left palm.

I fingered this ring while we drove.

I'd never met his parents. They died before I was born. His mother of Parkinson's disease.

"My mama, she was sweet. She made me mashed-potato cones for snacks when I was young. We didn't have a lot of money."

In the summers between the last years of elementary school and junior high, he took the subway alone to Coney Island. In his navy blue shorts he dove off the pier and swam day after day. He'd read about Johnny Weissmuller, another Jew, who was a swimming star. If he could do it, my father could too. Hand over hand, he had a lone determination. By the time he arrived in high school in ninth grade, they let him use the school pool. Now he could swim in the late fall, through the dark months of winter, and on into spring. At seventeen he won the freestyle. None of his family attended the meet to see him slap the edge one moment before the kid from Tilden High. So close and tight was his win that the slap was like two consecutive sounds—slap! slap! my father's and the other boy's—but his was first. The coach reached down and pulled him out of the water to the roar of the Lincoln home crowd. My father was the champion—self-taught—in all of Brooklyn.

But when he talked about it there was no glory. It was just luck, he said.

But for me he was champion of the world. I loved his close effort, his power. When I was young, I watched him dive over and over into the ocean at Jones Beach. He taught me to swim. I'd stand on his shoulders, and when the great waves came, the two of us charged right into them, me on top, he on the bottom.

From age twelve to sixteen I attended summer camp and learned lake swimming. All four years I made tremendous effort in the swim meets, but no matter how hard I tried to be my father, I always came in second after a thin dark-haired girl from Queens.

We got a seat right away at John G.'s near a wooden column. "Dad, should we move? You don't have a view of the sea."

He shrugged. "I know it's there. I don't have to see it." He ordered his favorite: salami and eggs.

I had my camera.

He put his hand over the lens. "Not now."

"Oh, come on. I need photos of my model." I had drawn him often in the last five years. Mostly he had been in his large reclining chair in front of the TV and being still had come naturally now.

Recently I'd sold a portrait. I called to tell him.

"You're kidding. A woman bought it? How old is she?"

"Twenty-six."

"Send her a real picture of me, in the army. She can see how I really look. She paid that much? She must be in love with me."

"Dad, she liked *my painting*."

"Don't be silly. Give me her address. I'll send her a Christmas card. Forget it. I'll marry her." Then he paused. "Hey, what's my cut?"

He reached for the single yellow rose in a thin glass vase in the center of the table, held it next to his cheek, and posed. Just as I was about to click, he stuck out his tongue.

"C'mon, Daddy. Be serious."

"Why?"

"Because I need your good looks."

"Yes, I am handsome," he smiled, and I snapped.

"Now you." He seized the camera and handed me the flower.

I didn't like being photographed here in Florida. My hair in the humidity twirled, curled, and formed wisps where it wasn't supposed to. I tried to smile.

On our way out, we stopped for toothpicks at the cashier's counter. A full cup of pennies was offered for use in a gum ball machine that gave M&Ms. My father and I each put in a coin and filled our hands with colored candy that fell down a shoot. We walked out popping the candy in our mouths and rolling the toothpicks across our lips.

IT WAS NOT ALWAYS this sweet between us. Nine years earlier I had written him a long letter. "Did you ever wonder what my childhood looked like to me?" Well, of course, he hadn't, but I thought—after hours of group and individual therapy—to inform him.

"You never knocked before you entered my bedroom. You commented often at the dinner table about my young breasts, and you tried to kiss me on the lips in a way that made me uncomfortable. I carried constant anger around as a defense, to ward you off. You tried to peek at me when I was an adolescent, naked in the shower. I didn't feel safe. You called me gooney, made fun of my nose, the shadow on my upper lip, my eyebrows growing across the bridge of my nose."

I wrote him that he was a terrible father, never came to my school, never asked about my homework. Sure, once he rode bicycles with me for a Girl Scout cookout, and once he brought a hundred boxes of Scout cookies to the bar and handed them out instead of change for beer purchases. His customers were outraged. "You don't like mint? Here's a box of pecan sandies." He grabbed the one box away and gave the other. I won the award for the most cookies sold. I remembered once when I was nine, sitting at the edge of my bed engrossed in reading a book, he walked in, rubbed my head, and said with obvious pride, "You're reading again?"

But that was it, I wrote. I hated my childhood.

When he received my letter, he tried to call, but after I said briskly, "Write me. No more phone calls," I hung up.

Two weeks later I received a thin envelope addressed in my father's crooked hand. I imagined a gorilla gripping a pen. "I don't know what you're talking about, but don't worry. I'll never leave you."

That was exactly him. My father knew two things: determination and animal devotion. My father would be eternally loyal to me. I was his daughter. He was my father. For my whole life we would stand in relationship to each other. That was it. I knew I'd get no more.

But I did not give up. I wrote back, "Your letter's not good enough." My father had not treated his young daughter well, and my mother did not protect me.

As soon as I left home at eighteen, I tried to figure out what went on in my family. I attended college in Washington, D.C. Freshman students were offered free counseling. I quickly took advantage of it and made an appointment.

In this new city, both strange and wonderful, I turned at the entrance of a corner brownstone only blocks from the White House and walked into a dank waiting room. I whispered to the receptionist, "I'm supposed to see someone at two." I wanted to keep the secrets of my life sealed until I entered the inner sanctum of that therapist's office.

A woman wearing a beige skirt, white blouse, single strand of pearls, and short black heels beckoned me into her room and then pointed to a dark wooden seat across from her desk.

I began by telling her that my boyfriend and I had

broken up a little while ago. Sex between us had died out. But I had a new boyfriend, and I occasionally saw the old one. Lovemaking was hot again with the old one, but I was numb with the person I liked now.

I told her that these two men were my first sexual partners. I knew something felt askew and I sensed that somehow it had to do with my father.

"Well, what new technique is your old boyfriend doing that's turning you on?" She removed her eyeglasses, exhaled on one lens, and rubbed it with a tissue.

"He's not doing anything different." I was no Sigmund Freud, but I knew this therapist wasn't catching on. I was trying to tell her something about myself, about my history. My forehead furrowed. I wanted her to lead me into my subconscious—wasn't that what it was all about?

"Your old boyfriend must be doing something different. Otherwise, you wouldn't feel excited." She put her glasses back on.

I tried to tell her again how uncomfortable I felt around my father. I explained that I wanted to feel good with the person I was dating, not with the sideshow.

She insisted my old boyfriend had a new technique.

I gave up. "I'll have to think about it," I said. Then sarcasm slid off my tongue. "That's right," I snapped my fingers, "he was wearing my red underpants."

"There you go," she brightened. The problem was solved.

I slinked out of there, marched down the streets of the capital of our great country, stormed into my dormitory, and never went back to college counseling again.

After I graduated, I moved to Detroit to live with a boyfriend and tried therapy again at a free clinic. The man sitting opposite me was a foreign graduate student. He explained he was getting his Ph.D.

I told him my problem. "I can be turned on as long as I'm not involved. Become my boyfriend, and it's the end of sex." I was older now, more experienced at verbalizing the dilemma, but the basic phenomenon was the same.

"I understand." He had a clipped accent. "If you become close, you think it is your father. You are afraid of having sex with your father."

"Yeah," I said. We were getting somewhere. "So what should I do?"

"It's rather simple. If you let yourself imagine having sex with your father, you will no longer be afraid. We are only afraid of the unknown."

I nodded. I wanted badly to solve this.

"I can help you."

I was elated.

"Lie down." He pointed to a green vinyl couch with no arms or back. I slid onto it. "Close your eyes and envision what I say."

I relaxed and shut my eyes.

He proceeded. "Your father has walked into the room. He comes to you. Can you see that?"

"Uh-huh." My lids closed tighter, and I gripped my

hands into fists, but I went along with him. He was going to cure me.

I heard "the penis entering the vagina" in the staccato rhythm of English spoken as a second language. I was floating above the room. I had just met this psychologist, and we had genitals going in and out of each other—my father's, no less. I thought, well, this therapy is free. He can't take too much time with each client. He has to get down to business. He punctuated the words "penis" and "vagina" as he repeated them over and over. Did they talk about this stuff in Japan? Maybe he came here to learn special American techniques. My mind was working fast. I didn't want to know what my father's genitals looked like, much less felt like. I was trying, but I was nauseous. It wasn't working.

"Okay, open your eyes."

I popped up, and the vinyl tore from my skin.

"Well, how do you feel?"

"Is this what you're doing your dissertation on?" I was overly friendly, tapping my foot up and down. Then I blurted out, "I feel the same." In truth I felt much worse, withdrawn and wooden.

He lifted his eyebrows, glanced at the clock on the back wall. "Sorry. The session is up."

I walked out of there like a stiff puppet.

TWENTY YEARS LATER, I was almost forty; my life was full of Zen practice and writing. In fact, I was about to finish a novel, the most difficult thing I'd ever attempted.

The main character, a loose copy of myself, was sleeping with too many men right before her marriage. It was true in real life, but it wasn't believable. It didn't work in the fiction. I was slashing whole paragraphs.

Outside the cafés and libraries I wrote in, women were whispering "sexual abuse." People all over the country were meeting in incest survivor groups. Everywhere I went I saw a thick white book entitled *The Courage to Heal* on coffee tables, lining shelves of bookstores, on friends' desks. Did I want to drag that old dog out? Who had the time? I had learned to cope. Besides, nothing as radical as intercourse happened between me and my father. I just was uncomfortable with him. He was inappropriate with me. I had language now. I had "inappropriate." I had a novel to finish. I was a woman now of singular focus.

The snow was deep the Monday in January when I returned to my house tired. I did not lock my front door. I was an old hippie and liked to believe in trusting the world. Sometimes I forgot my keys in my car. A year before, my blue Rabbit was stolen, but I didn't learn. I made a grilled cheese sandwich for dinner and read in bed until I fell asleep.

Around one in the morning I heard a vague rattling, turned over in bed, and then suddenly sat bolt upright. A naked man with a hairy chest and a nylon stocking over his head was standing over me. I could see his large body clearly in the moonlight pouring through the window.

I let out a scream so loud I did not hear it, but it filled my entire body. I only felt pure silence, but the sound pierced the old thick-walled adobe. Neighbors slammed on lights and dashed open doors, and the naked man in an instant was gone. I ran to the back door and let Steve, Juan, and Linda in. Someone else had already called the police. We could hear a distant siren. We walked gingerly to the front of the house. No trace of his clothes anywhere, but he couldn't have grabbed everything that fast. The door was ajar. We held open the useless screen. Bare footprints in the snow ran to the left and were lost under the streaks of car tires in the street's slush. Did he come in naked? Walk to my front door bare-assed? It was freezing outside. He must have lived right nearby. He couldn't have walked nude down Galisteo Street in the cold checking for an unlocked door.

The police arrived and told us they'd been after this guy. He never touched the women. The door was always unlocked. He just gazed. He had repeated this weekly for the last three months.

I made a quick, logical conclusion: lock my door. Then I'd be safe. I couldn't afford to engage my imagination. I had to use it for the novel.

The next morning I marched out of the house only a half hour later than usual to the Galisteo Newsstand, where I wrote. I would let nothing deter me. But I couldn't ward off the awful feeling that I was being watched. That that naked man lived across the street, down the block, kitty-corner to my place. At the café I was okay; later in my locked house I felt secure. It was the distance between the two that was terrorizing.

A month and a half later I finished my first draft. Then my close reserve exploded. That man was like my father! He never touched me; he just looked. I marched over to the rape crisis center and joined an abuse group.

These women were not like me. My father didn't do what their fathers, brothers, uncles, aunts, mothers, babysitters did to them. The walls of the room were a sickening green. Usually I loved groups, especially after the loneliness of writing each day, but I was squirming in my chair. I hated this meeting. I remembered how cute, funny my father was.

The frizzy-haired woman with large glasses across from me described how she shaved her pubic hair when it first came out so no one could see she was maturing. My face fell. I did the same thing. My sister had seen the thin downy first strands while we were in the bathroom, and she'd announced it at dinner. Then my father would try to walk in on me after a shower, so he too could see.

I didn't lock the door then either, and if I did, it was easy to pick the lock with an unbent paper clip. I learned early locks were useless. My puberty was filled with yelling at my father to shut the door, holding a pink towel in front of myself. I cut my pubic hair so my sister would shut her mouth. But I could not also cut off my breasts, the forming curve of my hips. My adolescence was an agony. I was the last girl in my seventh grade to get a bra, to wear nylons. I never wore jewelry, lipstick, eye shadow. I did not want to be noticed by the man in our house.

A pale woman in light green pedal pushers and high brown boots spoke next. She told how she tried at all costs to avoid being in a room alone with her father. I could hardly breathe. I'd come down the stairs from the bedroom, go out the front door, and come in the back to go up to the kitchen, all to avoid walking through the living room, where my father sat on the couch.

"This will be our text." The leader of the group held up that big white book I'd seen everywhere. Each chapter ended with a writing assignment. We were to come back the next week with our notebooks.

I began to write in a thin green one. As my pen scratched across the page, the world of my childhood started to coalesce. Too many things I'd forgotten, never uttered I was now describing, and then it was affirmed by the experience of these women. A case was being built. I wasn't crazy. Something did happen.

Each week no matter what the assignment, I'd open that notebook and scream with my pen, "Fuck you, fuck you, fuck you." A whole book filled with little more than those two words. In group I watched women who'd never written before take satisfaction in describing a certain dress, meal, house.

The leader would encourage. "Very vivid. Good. Good."

My turn would come. I was an inarticulate banshee. I couldn't believe this man I had loved with all my young heart had been so disrespectful to me, treated me like a "broad," a "hussy," behaved as though I didn't matter, as though I wasn't his daughter. He didn't love me. He couldn't. Then I'd stop. What about *his* mean father, his childhood? He didn't know any better. It was the fifties—he could only see women as sex objects. I'd make excuses. But I was his flesh and blood. My mind whirled. I couldn't put the two together. "How could you be my father and handle me like this?" I'd howl in my pillow at night, "But I was your daughter. I was your daughter."

Then I'd stop trying to understand; I just burned. I cried in uncontrollable convulsions several times a day as though I were vomiting. I felt my thin ten-year-old-girl legs under the kitchen table as we ate dinner and he made snide comments when an uncle was visiting. "Hey, Nat has baby hairs under her arms. Come over and show it." I had on a sleeveless shirt. I couldn't see any in the mirror. I'd show them they were mistaken. My father held up my arm, and they peered close. "See?" my father pointed with his thick forefinger, just grazing the two frail growths. I pulled away and ran to the medicine-chest mirror to look. Even in the dead heat of July I wore sleeves after that.

Where was my mother? This wasn't clandestine mistreatment; we were at the dinner table, for heaven's sake. She was busy spooning the onion gravy over the pot roast;

she was taking her apron off to sit down; she was reaching into the refrigerator for some milk. I had no protector. Everything was in the open, and no one stopped it. Was the rest of the house occupied by ghosts? Where was everyone?

But I loved him. He taught me to swim.

Whenever I'd soften, I'd think, Hitler had a bad childhood. Was that an excuse? It would reignite me. But I'd also watch the depth of my own doubt, how I wanted to shut off what I didn't want to know.

I experienced all my withheld rage in my legs. I wanted to run as hard as I could as far as I could from that house in Farmingdale, New York. In Santa Fe I started a women's running club and found a coach, who encouraged us to run like animals. My desire was to scorch the track, burn up my past; instead, I was the slowest, most quietly faithful one in the group. Wherever I had to travel to teach writing, Manhattan, Kansas City, Boulder, I'd put on those rubber shoes and pound the streets with my feet.

The big word I learned was "boundary." "Here's where I end. You begin over there. Daddy, get the hell out of my way." I was experiencing the death of my father, of some dream I was brought up to believe about daddies and their daughters.

One night as soon as the meeting at the rape crisis center was over, I dashed over to the Zia Diner and shoved meat loaf and mashed potatoes down my throat. I noticed a familiar woman at another booth. We locked eyes for a moment, almost nodded, then looked away. Just ten minutes earlier we'd been divulging our deepest pains. Outside we acted as if we had nothing in common. Camaraderie or closeness was unbearable. I stayed distant from the other women. I was frightened to get too close.

No one in the group knew I was a writer. The truth was I don't think I ever even heard the writing topics that were assigned. Only anger fueled my hand. And grief. This was the end of the world. The statistics were startling: one out of every four children, then I'd hear one out of six. The numbers stopped mattering. I was learning something true and mean about the world. Rabbis, priests, parents, siblings, cousins, teachers—this was oppression, close up and personal. And insidious—it quietly ruled and ruined lives. Just twenty years ago no one could help me. Therapists were ignorant. It was important for women to help each other, to hear the stories and recognize ourselves. The process was slow and painful, but I was no longer under my father's thumb.

For the next year my mother wrote, "Dear Natalie, we loved you so much. We didn't mean to make a mistake," and then in another letter, "We did the best we could," and "This isn't fair."

Six months later they sent an old photo they'd blown up as a gift: Rhoda, in a diaper, is one year old with dark big eyes and a head of curly hair, sitting on my mother's left knee. My mother, with full lips, bright eyes, and thick hair, is looking down lovingly at her. And I, at four in a plaid dress, barrette in my hair, am leaning on her right leg, trying to get her attention.

All that photo did was ignite my wrath. My mother never saw me, and it was right there in the framed picture. She was getting off easy in the letters I sent. She had basically ignored me for my whole childhood. Simple questions—What yellow school bus do I take to first grade? What do I wear to school? How do I find the classroom?—were never answered, as though she were on drugs and never heard me. And in fact, she often was. Sleeping pills, Valium, diet pills were dispensed liberally by her brother, the doctor. I mustered a confident air, but was shattered inside. Finally at the end of the first day at Main Street Elementary, I broke down sobbing, my face hidden in my arms leaning on the wooden desk. Already there was an acknowledgment that I was on my own, set adrift in a huge world at an early age.

I think even worse than being taunted by my father was being neglected by my mother. It created no affirmation of my existence. It was probably even a deeper wound, but I wasn't ready to take on both parents at once.

I thought, all my work, and this was their response? They enclosed a note, "See how happy we were?"

"No, I don't," I wrote back. How blind could they be?

I did not see them for another six months. The last letter from my mother read, "Please, Nat, let's go back to before this all began, when we were all content."

Content! I crumpled up the paper and tossed it in the wastebasket. More time passed. My parents were never going to understand.

I WAS AT A RECONCILIATION RETREAT in New York with Thich Nhat Hanh, the Vietnamese Buddhist monk. In 1968 Martin Luther King Jr. nominated him for the Nobel Peace Prize. Besides regular practitioners, Vietnam vets were invited to attend. Thirty came. Thay, as we called this spiritual teacher, wanted to meet with these American soldiers who had been at war with his country. It was 1991. He felt they still suffered terribly, and he wanted to tell them to forgive themselves, let go, go on, help someone now, no matter what happened in the past.

Many of these vets had not seen a Vietnamese person since they were in the war in Asia. Scores of them hadn't had a night's sleep since they left the jungle. Some were just getting off alcohol and drugs. A few hadn't touched another human being since they returned.

I was asked to lead twelve vets in a group discussion. We went off to a grassy knoll. I was the only woman. I asked the man to my right with close-cut hair, a mustache, wearing army fatigues to begin. "Share how it feels to be here."

I had no training for this, but I'd been a teacher and a meditator for a long time. I'd run groups, but most important, I'd seen into my own family's darkness.

I listened patiently, evenly, quietly. I did not comment. I just let people talk. Once the ground of acceptance had been laid, I was the silent witness. As soon as the men began to share, they could not stop. Every once in a while they glanced over at me. Was I wincing at their tales?

They became more bold, divulged more horrifying stories, but I wasn't judging, nor was I shocked.

The men told me how grateful they were that I could listen. It was my turn to speak. "I've seen what close relatives, families, people you're supposed to trust can do to each other. If that is possible, why should we be surprised what people do to others they have never met, people we think are foreigners from another land."

A gray-eyed man sitting directly across from me chimed in, "'Nam looked like a party compared to what went on in my family in Boston before I enlisted at eighteen."

I nodded. I was no longer that bookish girl with hair pulled straight back, ending in a ponytail, who still carried a schoolbag in high school, silent, hiding from the bewildering truth of her family. The inner work I had been doing about my father was necessary. I knew that. It wasn't about sex alone, but an essential stance I had in relation to the world.

IN SEPTEMBER OF THAT YEAR, my friend Carol, the dermatologist from the Twin Cities, called, and we planned a trip to Prague for three weeks. We left in November.

Something about travel in a foreign country loosens your perceptions. As we walked back and forth across the ancient bridge over the Vltava River, many thoughts came to me.

I remembered hearing a story fifteen years earlier about my second cousins Eric, seventeen, and David, eighteen. Neither of them had a father: one father had died too young, and the other had abandoned his family. Even though these two boys were his blood, I doubt that my father was trying to be paternally helpful; more likely he was bored when he made his offer at a family gathering. "Hey," he turned to them, a cup of tea in his hand, two rugalach on his plate. "It's not too late. Let's hit Aqueduct for a couple of races. I'll show you boys the real world."

They jumped in the car and turned the clover onto the Long Island Expressway. Both cousins had driver's licenses, but my father manned the car. He was their great-uncle Buddy, older than history (he must have been sixty), and he had a predilection for driving slow, very, very slow. He was going forty in the left lane, cars whizzing by on the right.

"C'mon, Uncle Buddy, we'll never get there," David whined from the passenger seat.

"Never mind. Look at the scenery. You live in Connecticut. Enjoy Long Island." He flicked his cigar ashes in the open tray.

"We'll never make it," Eric from the backseat chimed in. David turned around, they looked at each other, and they both fell over laughing.

"No rush. No rush. The horses are waiting for us. Eric, you're a smart boy. Aren't you going to Harvard? You should know speed is for the astronauts."

They pulled into the full parking lot and found a spot far from the entrance. They could hear the cheers in the stands. Suddenly, Uncle Buddy's legs were in motion, the slow man driving a car could really move in the parking lot, the glint off the chrome only exciting him more.

"But I'm under age!" Eric yelled after his great-uncle's back.

My father stopped dead, then turned. "Eric, a smart boy like you, how could you do this to me? C'mon, let's see what I've got in the trunk."

He pulled out baggy trousers. "Here, put them on." He plopped a fedora on his head. It fell below his eyes.

My father stood back. "I don't know," he mused. Then he bent down, picked up two handfuls of dirt, and rubbed it on Eric's cheeks.

"Now walk with a limp like you've got arthritis. No one will stop you."

Eric began to protest.

"Let's go." My father charged ahead.

The authorities grabbed Eric immediately. "What kind of joke is this?"

My father was aching for a winning ticket. He had no time. He ignored the police and spoke directly to his great-nephew. "I'll tell you what." He stuck his hand in his pocket. "Here's the keys. You go back and wait in the car. David and I will just watch two races. We'll bet on one for you."

It was dusk, many races later, when they returned. My father had only won one out of eight. They weaved among the field of cars.

"Where did we park?" my father called to David as they fanned out.

"There's the car." David pointed in the distance at a blue Buick.

"But where's Eric?" They rushed toward the vehicle.

He was crumpled in the backseat. My father knocked on the glass with his knuckles. Eric didn't rouse. He knocked harder.

My father went for his keys and then remembered Eric had them. "Oh, my God, he locked the doors."

"Jeez, it was sweltering all day," David whispered. "There's no open windows. Do you think he's alive?"

"Sure. C'mon," my father jumped on the trunk and rocked the car.

"You bang," he ordered David. "Son of a gun, that kid can sleep."

Eric slowly lifted his head as though he was moving it through wet cement. The first thing he saw was my father's face, his nose smashed against the window. "Open the door."

David on the other side of the car raised his fists high

in the air. "Uncle Buddy did it again—he raised the dead from the living."

My father peered across the car hood, "Kid, you got it all backwards. Your Uncle Buddy got the sleeping to wake up."

The car door swung open. My father jumped in and lit the ignition. "Now, you boys, tell both your mothers you had a very educational time. That your uncle could have been a professor, why even a doctor of philosophy."

They both started to jeer.

"I did go the College of Hard Knocks, you know."

I smiled. It was all there: the thoughtlessness, the inconsideration. Oh, but was he fun! My whole childhood I wanted so badly for him to play with me, but I was a girl. I only interested him in narrow ways.

By the time I reached Prague, I had not seen my parents in over three years. During the whole trip one thought plagued me: "Two people on this earth look like me, carry the same genes."

I returned to the States determined to reconnect. My parents would never respond to my accusations the way I wanted them to. My father was a disrespectful bully, and he could be a cruel tease. But something had turned for me. I knew he would never mistreat me again. I had withdrawn, and he could not bear that. He had no savvy about psychological things, but he did not want to lose me. In a way I did not wholly understand, by having drawn an invisible line he could not cross, I also gave him freedom from his own confused boundaries.

I called on a Saturday night, and my father and I were soon arguing: Who will visit first?

"So what you're saying is you'll never visit us again?" he screamed into the phone. "I'm hanging up." He slammed the phone down. My mother was on another phone. I was breathing heavily. I felt the old hate, but I remembered my vow to reconnect. "Mom, tell him to get back on."

He got back on. You could feel the electric rage between us, but deeper there was determination. "Natalie, you know that vacuum cleaner you want?" he managed to say through gulps of air, "Well, I think you should get a Hoover."

"Do you need it for carpet or wood floors?" He proceeded. He spoke for three full minutes about cleaner parts. He was desperate to keep the connection going. My father was a vacuum salesman before he bought the bar and was now using anything he knew.

I agreed I wanted a stand-up, then no, maybe he was right, an Electrolux might be better.

He talked on, so thick with appliance details I was certain I was in training to become a salesman, just like he had been.

Then he paused, "Don't buy one. Wait. We'll come to New Mexico in May, and I'll help you choose one."

I understood: no psychology talk. This is how my

father communicated. This man, however ignorantly, must love me.

Five months later they flew out.

My parents wasted no time. They launched right back into my spiritual education on the second day of their visit after three years of being apart. That was when my father belted out "Hello Dolly" on the porch using my meditation bell. No Zen master was able to smash false notions the way my parents could. I saw I still was gullible at the core.

It was exactly right that I had talked about Te-shan at that conference. I was merely acting out his dilemma in another dimension. He had the tea-cake woman at the side of the road. I had Syl and Bud from Brooklyn, who were so enlightened they had no idea they were even awake. They were much too busy befuddling me, revealing my ignorance to myself.

On the third afternoon we drank some lemonade in the kitchen—my father preferred his root beer or at least Canada Dry ginger ale—but he was attempting good behavior, and he tried to be polite. He drank his glass of lemonade.

When my mother went off into the bedroom to call my sister, my father leaned in like a coconspirator. "So tell me, Nat, what was wrong—all those letters? Really. I didn't get it. Were you on drugs?"

I'd just taken a gulp of lemonade. The glass was at my mouth. Full of disbelief, I burst out laughing, spraying the drink all over my hand.

"No, really, you broke our hearts." He tapped my forearm. "What kind of trouble were you in?"

All the thousands of dollars I had spent in therapy— the intimate hours of study of my family flashed before me. Useless, all useless. "Well, Dad—" I began.

He cut me off. "You went to a psychiatrist?" He was in shock.

I corrected him. "A psychologist."

He waved that off. "What's the difference? Why, our whole family's nutty. You could have asked me."

Then he moved in closer to ensure that no one else could hear. "You didn't talk about me? What did he say?"

"Dad, it was a woman. She said—"

He didn't wait for an answer. He could not imagine a woman doctor. "Nat, I had a lousy childhood. My father was a mean son of a bitch. With Jews at the time we'd call our fathers 'Pop.' In second grade, in the public schools I heard them say 'Dad' and 'Daddy.'" He brushed his forehead with the palm of his hand. "So I tried it out. When my father came home from work, I said, 'Hi, Dad,' and he looked me straight in the face and said, 'What? You're a sissy?'"

My father shook his head. "We were miserable, but we didn't *talk* about it." He gulped down the last of his lemonade.

Just then my mother walked in and sensed something was amiss. "What have you been talking about?"

"Oh, we had a little friendly father-daughter exchange." He was proud of himself.

My mother looked from one to the other of us nervously. She wanted things to go smoothly.

I interjected, "Joan Mitchell, an American painter who lived in France most of her life, is being shown nearby."

My father brightened. For some reason he liked paintings. He never could believe people could make realistic pictures on canvas. He thought it was a wonder. "The artist came all the way from France to visit?"

"No, but the paintings did."

"Sure, let's go," he said.

My mother was only relieved the subject had changed; also she liked to pretend an interest in culture. After all, her brother was a doctor, and besides, it was an excuse to switch into another outfit. "Give me just a minute."

Walking into the new yellow stuccoed building on Read Street, we were immediately hit with canvases, each as big as a small Volkswagen, splashed with color.

Stepping over to the first one, my father peered closely at the oils. Then he stepped back. "Hey, Nat," he said excitedly. "I know how the painter made it. He filled a cannon with paint and then let it rip."

"Very funny," I said and stepped to the next one, too engrossed to bother correcting his gender assumptions again.

He followed after me, and we looked together at two more. My mother had wandered off.

"I've seen enough," he said. "My knees hurt." My father's legs, after thirty years of standing behind the bar serving drinks, felt tired now. "Find me a chair. I'll just sit and wait."

"A chair is in the back down the hall," the woman behind the desk pointed.

"I'll find it." He trailed off.

I couldn't believe I was getting to see so many of these pictures in person. I was in the process of writing a book about painting, and Mitchell was one of the women painters I had discovered and admired the most.

I came to the end of the show. Out of the corner of my eye I saw my mother heading for the bathroom.

I stepped into the gallery library, a soft gray–carpeted room, and my father was so intently bent over a book on his lap, he didn't hear me come in. I peeked over his right shoulder. He was looking at an abstract pastel by Mitchell, touching the page with his forefinger.

He was suddenly aware of me. "Nat, tell me. What's this a picture of? I'm looking and looking, and I can't figure it out. Is it a tree? A house? I can't find anything."

"Dad," I placed my hand on his shoulder, "it's abstract. It's not supposed to represent anything."

He did not pursue this. His moment of curiosity was over. "You done? Let's go. I've had enough." He slammed the book shut.

We met my mother in the hall, and as we headed out, I asked the same woman behind the desk, "How much?"

She glanced up. "Two fifty."

My father caught the number and was working it around in his brain. We stepped outside and blinked. Though it was late afternoon, the New Mexico light was penetrating.

"Well, I guess that's fair," my father said. "There's a lot of paint and those big canvases. The materials could easily cost that much."

"Dad, she meant two hundred and fifty *thousand*."

We were crossing the street. His face fell. For the first time ever, he could not respond. This was too much to grasp, too beyond his reach. As we drove to the restaurant for dinner, he was totally silent, looking straight ahead out the windshield.

I enjoyed this moment. My father was stumped.

AFTER THAT VISIT in Santa Fe, I traveled down to Florida three months later. I knew they were aging, and I wanted to see them whenever I could. My mother mysteriously moved from room to room in her nightgown. I supposed she was not feeling well, but I did not worry so much about her. She often seemed distracted.

The last time I'd visited—before the letters began— I'd invited her repeatedly to come to lunch with me in Palm Beach, just the two of us. When she finally agreed and I took her to a swanky restaurant I thought she'd enjoy, also to impress her that her daughter could afford ten-dollar salads, she said over and over, "I have to get home to your father."

"Why?" I entreated. "He's fine on his own."

"I don't like to be away too long."

Two hours was too long? I wouldn't be visiting for another six months. The continual message I received throughout my childhood was I wasn't worth taking time for. Here it was again being stamped on my forehead.

The other thing she did at this luncheon was comment, on every third bite of food, "This is robbery. We could have gone to a place near our house that gives you twice as much for half the price."

We, of course, never approached the simple conversation I longed for: a question or show of interest in what I was doing or how I felt. Nor did she ever share anything about herself.

As soon as we arrived home, she dashed to the back bedroom to call my sister across the country. Together they commiserated about the poor restaurant choice I made. They were as tight as thieves, and I was left out. It was an old family story I experienced in a hundred ways. I stood at the front door diminished to insignificance.

NOTHING HAD EVER BEEN PHYSICALLY wrong with my mother before. My mother's people seemed to live forever. Sam Edelstein, her father, died at ninety-two and her mother, Rose, at ninety-four. But I often thought she could use some of that old-fashioned psychology I had swallowed in gulps. Simple things like: What do you *feel*? What were your dreams, Mom, before you were submerged by your overbearing husband? What is it *you* want to eat when you look at a menu, rather than first checking to see what everyone else is going to order? But I left well enough alone this time. I was tired of being the only one to stir the deep waters. Besides, I enjoyed this new connection with my father. My mother seemed oddly relieved when we left the house and went off on our own.

On the second afternoon of my visit, my father and I picked up the newspaper and drove to my hotel. We planned to go to the races, and he was perusing the Daily Racing Form at the small kitchen table.

"I'm betting on the first two races. Only two. Read me the names. I have an intuition about these things," I said to him.

"Humph," my father let out a long breath.

"C'mon, read them."

"Nightline. Cosmos. Baby's Head. Long Whistle. Vermont Air. Last Puzzle. Kiddin' Around. Blue Will. Zumbro."

I twisted up my face, conjuring the winner. Zumbro had snap. Plus I used to have a boyfriend who lived near the Zumbro River in Minnesota.

"You gotta be kidding. That horse has the worst odds."

"Exactly. When he wins, I'll win big."

"You don't know what you're talking about. Where's the trash?" He threw in a banana peel. "We don't have to bother going to the track. You might as well dump your money in the garbage."

I insisted I knew what I was doing.

My father was half disgusted—he took gambling seriously. Then something big came over him. "I'll tell you what! Let's bet on which horse falls down first." Our eyes locked across the table—a hiatus like a sensation of space in a haiku stopped us dead. We burst into hard laughter. My father's head dropped to the table. He leaned on his arms, drool forming at the corner of his mouth. Everything shimmered, shook: the window over the sink, the burners on the stove, the refrigerator, our water glasses on the table. I was almost choking.

For moments we were free of aches and pains, even free of the weight of the roles of father and daughter. We were in Florida, a whole new state from New York, and we'd known each other for fifty years.

In great delight I rose up and grabbed a blank piece of hotel stationery from the counter. With a black pen, I wrote: "I, Benjamin Goldberg, have received five dollars from Natalie Goldberg, and I will bet it on number nine in the first race. If I neglect to bet it and Zumbro wins, I owe Natalie the money at twenty to one."

I pushed the paper across the yellow Formica table and said, "Sign this. I'm going swimming. I'm not going to the racetrack. I'll give you the five."

He read my formal printing.

"Give me the pen." He reached out his arm. "BULL SHIT" he wrote in caps in his shaky hand, and then signed and handed it back. He was gleeful. "I haven't laughed

like that in I don't know when. You know, I'm not going
to the track either." His eyes were gleaming. He had
taken a great leap. He suddenly saw things in a whole
new way.

MY FATHER HAD WON AND LOST hundreds, probably
thousands, of dollars gambling on horses. My mother said
we would have been rich, if it weren't for his betting. I
never quite believed how wealthy we would have been.

One Passover when I was eleven, we were in Brooklyn with my mother's oldest brother, the doctor. Paintings
from Europe were on the walls, and we passed matzo to
each other wrapped in a fresh linen napkin. The meal
had an elegant dignity. My grandmother, who lived with
us, had made the gefilte fish. Just two days earlier the
fresh carp had been swimming in our bathtub. Grandma
was proud of her son, and he adored her cooking, put
extra beet horseradish on his plate. And those plates!
Gold trimmed with a royal blue circle. Even as a young
girl I knew the plates were imported from across the
Atlantic. Was it England? Belgium? I could never remember. We munched on moist sponge cake, small
chocolate truffles for dessert.

I was happy in the special blue dress I wore. Here in
Flatbush we were surrounded by Jews, our people.
Passover was close to Easter, and at home on Long
Island we lived in an all-Catholic neighborhood. To feel
comfortable back in Farmingdale we wore Easter hats,

white ones with red ribbons, and new spring coats with black velvet trim.

But here in Flatbush, when dessert was over, we put on our new garb to stroll to Martense Street, just ten blocks away, to my father's relatives for a little visit, maybe a second Passover dessert. My mother didn't come with us. My sister and I each held one of my father's hands. At different intervals Rhoda skipped, and I wouldn't step on the sidewalk cracks. My father wore a tan overcoat, unbuttoned, flapping open, and a brown fedora. He was moving fast, not paying a lot of attention to us. This was not unusual, but still it was special to have time alone with him.

We rang the bell to the upstairs half of the white clapboard duplex, and the ring came back to us. My father quickly turned the knob. Aunt Lil, with her dyed flamingred hair, my father's oldest sister, along with Uncle Sam, his oldest brother, and Junie, my skinny red-headed, redfreckled cousin, who was somehow becoming beautiful as she grew older, all leaned out the door above the long brown-carpeted stairway, shouting, "It's Buddy. C'mon up," and we dashed up the flight, jumping into their arms.

Here in Aunt Lil's living room were big print couches you could flop on and dishes of pretzels, potato chips, and hard candies in twists of bright foil paper. I quickly unwrapped a caramel and popped it into my mouth, grabbed for a fistful of greasy chips. I knew no one here would notice or reprimand me.

My father's relations all seemed larger than life. Aunt Lil's hair was long and wild, pulled back in a barrette, and her laugh was full of gusto. Her husband, Uncle Seymour, had wavy short black hair and a full face. Something about him? I never could put my finger on it. He wasn't unfriendly. He just seemed awkward in the yellow nylon shirts he always wore. What was going on with him? He never laughed like the rest of them, only smiled, not showing any teeth. (We found out years later after he died that at that very same time he was with us, he had a whole second, hidden family with two sons, living in a suburb of Newark, New Jersey.) But my thoughts couldn't linger on him. Aunt Rae, the other sister, the one with the nose job, was now bringing out from the back room Easter baskets for me and Rhoda. Yippee! I snapped off the head of the chocolate bunny and shoved it in my mouth. All the polite manners I exercised at Uncle Manny's could be done away with here. I acted as though they hadn't served a thing over there. This freedom was dizzying.

Aunt Rae lived downstairs with Uncle Sam, but he wasn't there very much. Neither of them ever married. Though I heard that once Aunt Rae ran off to Florida when she was seventeen with a no-good, but Aunt Lil, the older sister, went down to get her and had the marriage annulled. The legend was that Rae and Lil had great legs, real sets of gams, and even my father had gorgeous legs. My mother didn't. All legs would have been the same to me—I was an unsuspecting child who even at eleven did not know about menstrual periods—but value was constantly being put on body parts in my family. Often I heard how one cousin had long piano fingers, a distant uncle had a good nose but a blunt chin, and another relative's lips were too thin.

My Aunt Rae sat opposite us on a stuffed chair, her ankles crossed, one hand holding the wrist of the other. She was smiling, half at us, half in her own dream. Once a few years back when we were alone, she told me about all the beaus she had had, and she showed me costume jewelry they had given her. I cocked my head to look more closely at her nose job. I knew my father loved her. She was the one who looked after him, the youngest in the family. Once as a joke as we were saying good-bye, he stuck his tongue in her mouth. She pulled back and said in a motherly tone, "Buddy, stop that."

Aunt Rae used to get paid to dance with men at a bar in Manhattan. They would buy her drinks, but the bartender only gave her water, my family explained to me. Why would someone treat her to water? I wondered. Everyone seemed relieved when she landed a job selling nylons at a new Alexander's downtown. Then something about Uncle Sam making up the difference in her salary.

During that long summer afternoon in Brooklyn she slipped me peeks at photos, kept in a hidden pocket of her purse, in which she sat at a nightclub table, her flower-patterned dress cut low, two or three idiot men leering at her and gripping whiskey glasses.

I peered at the pictures, then back at her. I understood at an early age that my Aunt Rae was a truly innocent woman with a big and simple heart who did not question the hearts of the men she encountered. Contrary to family opinion, my Aunt Rae seemed fond of her late twenties and thirties when she was beautiful and men desired her.

She was unerringly sweet to me. I started in on the white jelly beans. After all, who else remembered to give me an Easter basket?

I glanced over at Uncle Sam, Aunt Lil, and my father, who were huddled at a corner of the dining room table, gesturing wildly and telling jokes. My aunt hit my father on the upper arm with her open palm, "Oh, Buddy," her eyes full of tears, but she wasn't crying. She was laughing.

I began to eat all the greens, then the yellows.

I watched Uncle Sam. He was always the oddest, with his wiry body, broken Yiddish, mismatched clothing, and loud voice. He was the family genius. My father enlisted twice for active duty in World War II, so his older brother didn't have to go once.

I heard the story many times that money ran short and Uncle Sam couldn't finish medical school, so he became a druggist instead. Bored selling Chiclets and iron pills to old people in the area, he mixed chemicals and tried them on his own body. My parents showed him my A's in math and science, and he offered to put me through pharmacy school when I grew up. My mother raised her eyebrows. This was a good deal, but a girl pharmacist? Shouldn't she be a teacher?

I was curious about Uncle Sam. I had often cajoled my mother into telling me about him. After all, I reasoned to her, I needed to know what a pharmacist's life would be like. My mother put her erect index finger in front of her lips, indicating the secrecy of this story she was about to tell. Above the pharmacy was a two-bedroom flat he rented to a night salesman and his wife, whose name was Charlotte. She was lonely when Murray was away and often came down to talk to Sam, who worked behind the counter till eleven at night in a white button-down shirt. They talked uninterrupted for hours, because the old customers stayed home at night. She confessed to Sam that she still loved salads with marshmallows in them, and she swore she heard crickets once in the middle of winter in upstate New York, back in high school, as she walked home from a dance.

Sam told her about the way his mom used to cook only kosher food, and then he told her what kosher food was, how the pink dishes were for dairy only and the white ones were for meat. On Friday nights they ate braided egg bread and wore small skullcaps. He could speak a language called Yiddish and read Hebrew, where the sentences started from the wrong side of the page.

I wanted my mother to keep going. I didn't care if this had anything to do with my future trade. She hesitated and then continued.

Sam was strange to her, but night after night, talking a counter width away from each other, they fell in love. She was twenty-five and he was already thirty, never having had a girlfriend before.

And there was friendship, my mother said. They'd go off fishing together, and they whistled. Charlotte in sneakers, no socks, rolled up dungarees, and Uncle Sam in old white shorts, shirtless, those few small hairs coming out where his heart was.

This was where my mother stopped the story, but I begged more details out of her.

Murray had no whiff of the affair at first or else didn't care. Sam, who was spending more and more time in Manhattan with Charlotte, rather than at his duplex in Brooklyn that he shared with Aunt Rae, finally rented the second bedroom from Charlotte's husband, Murray, in the apartment above the pharmacy that they actually rented from him.

"Do you get it?" My mother paused in the narrative. It was so *meshugas* (which meant "crazy").

So Uncle Sam spent nights with Charlotte while Murray worked, and Murray spent days with her while Sam worked. Everyone grew comfortable together, like old shoes. Sundays they sat around the table, Charlotte frying eggs and bacon, toasting bagels, and Murray and Sam reading the paper, throwing out facts about the mayor, Washington, and the low temperature the day before.

I leaned my head on my hand and tried to act nonplussed, so she'd go on. But I needn't have worried. My mother was lost in the story now. Nothing could have stopped her.

In the summers Sam closed the pharmacy, and he and Charlotte spent two months at Twin Oaks, the old dilapidated mansion on the south shore of Long Island that his family a long time ago had bought for a song. Murray would come out on weekends.

It was at Twin Oaks when I knew Charlotte and Sam the best. I was five or six, and I remembered the smell of turpentine, the wooden ladder, the white hens in the tall grass as Sam and Charlotte painted the trim on the endless summer home. Charlotte and I sat in the white kitchen at Twin Oaks making up songs about Uncle Sam, while Charlotte cut up carrots for coleslaw with the tan dog Fluffy at her feet. I never knew Charlotte's last name.

My mother continued. Charlotte must have known Sam was nuts, or odd or temperamental, but she loved him. Once when Uncle Sam heard raccoons running on top of the roof, he ran for a gun and shot at them through the bedroom ceiling. White plaster filled in cracks in the old wooden floor and covered everything for days.

In Uncle Sam's bedroom there was at least a thousand

dollars' worth of hi-fi equipment next to a thin mattress on the floor. Sam was wild about classical music. He turned the hi-fi so loud Dad would run up the stairs—

I interjected, "Didn't I follow after him? Wasn't I real young?"

Yes, she nodded, and went on. He banged on the door, but Uncle Sam couldn't hear. He wanted Charlotte to listen to a new record he'd bought, and when it was done he turned to her and whispered, "Did you like that?"

My mother moved her head closer to mine, and there was urgency in her telling.

One January they went to Carnegie Hall to hear a live performance. He was loaded, but he was so cheap he would spend the money for tickets only once a year. After the concert was over, Sam stood up in the balcony, put two fingers in his mouth, and let out a shrill whistle like an ump at a Dodgers' game. He stuck thumbs-up with his other hand and shouted, "Atta boy, Isaac!"

"You know who Isaac was, don't you?" My mother didn't wait for me to answer. "Only Isaac Stern, the greatest violinist in the world." Just then I noticed a raised mole on my mother's upper lip.

She moved deeper into the story. Then he helped Charlotte put her coat over her pink satin dress—can you imagine wearing that to a concert?—and, with rubbers on their feet, they walked through the winter slush to the subway. Over and over Uncle Sam heard the concert in his head.

Eventually Murray died and Charlotte and Uncle Sam married in an Israeli restaurant—suddenly my reverie was interrupted. "C'mon, girls. It's time to go." My father stood up from Aunt Lil's table.

Just as we were hugging everyone good-bye, my father said aloud, "Last week at the races I made an extra five hundred dollars, but I didn't tell Sylvia." He said it to show off to his older siblings. I even understood that then, but all I cared about was that he betrayed my mother, whom we left, still visiting her brother, our Uncle Manny, several city blocks away.

"Oh, Buddy, you shouldn't," my Aunt Lil said.

I didn't say a word as we walked back to my uncle's, but as soon as the door was opened, I ran to my mother, cupped my hand over her ear, and whispered, "Daddy won five hundred dollars and didn't tell you."

I dashed into the bathroom and vomited my Easter candy into the toilet.

As we drove the hour out to Farmingdale, huddled into the Buick, all six of us, including my grandmother and grandfather, my mother didn't say a word, but I felt vindicated anyway. I had held a rage beneath the surface, and now I had proof of his violation.

Usually, my mother had no problem screaming in front of the immediate family but, oddly, it was quiet in the house for the next three days. I forgot about the whole incident.

On the fourth day, it was a Wednesday—I remember

clearly because that was the day each week after school I went to my Girl Scout troop meeting—I met my father on the walkway leading up to the front door of our split level. He worked nights; it was a little after five and he was running late. When he saw me, his face turned ugly. "Because of you, your mother and I almost divorced." Then he belted me across the face with his fist. My head jerked back, but I quickly turned and looked straight at him. I did not utter a word. I was no longer young. He hurried past me to his car. I marched stunned into the house and sat down at the kitchen table, in the center of which my grandmother was about to place a platter of lamb chops. I silently ate the mashed potatoes she lovingly put back into the skin.

My father had never hit me before. He was a big man and doubled as the bouncer in his own bar. Years later he told me that that incident in front of our house unraveled him. He expected me to burst out crying.

Even at eleven I was honing myself to meet him head-on and stand up. My father had an inner power that could recognize the integral power in others. I think he recognized the crude beginnings of mine that day.

ON THE LAST NIGHT of my visit in Florida, I said goodbye to my mother. She still seemed removed, but when I asked her about it, she said she'd just been tired. My mother and I hugged. She told me to have a safe trip. My plane left early the next day.

My father drove me back to the hotel. At the first sign of any yellow light he braked. He timed it perfectly, so he didn't miss one red light. His driving was maddening.

As we sat in the car waiting for green, he gnawed on one end of an unlit Bering Plaza cigar. I could see he did not want to let me go. "Did I ever tell you about this one anti-Semite who came to the bar regularly in the early sixties."

Yes, he had told me, but I said, "Vaguely. Tell it to me again."

My father relished bitterness and revenge. "I turned green every time I handed this man a whiskey. The man talked of hebes and kikes and then ordered another drink on the rocks. I poured it like it was gasoline. I wanted to burn this man. He had a scar above his right eye, I remember. Weeks passed. This was a good-paying customer, but I tasted bile whenever this man stepped up to the barstool.

"You were, I think, in junior high school. One Saturday we visited Uncle Sam at the pharmacy in Manhattan."

I nodded. I remember licking a cone of coffee ice cream at the counter, when my father leaned over to his brother. By then my uncle's teeth were yellow and browned at the roots. He had a prominent skull that jutted out from his thin neck, and he wore a narrow mustache above almost invisible lips. He rolled down his white shirtsleeves as he listened to his only brother.

"Sam, I wanna get this anti-Semite. I don't want to do

him in—I only want to make him real uncomfortable. The son of a bitch."

My uncle's face was the color of putty in the gray light from the big front windows.

"Buddy, you have to be careful." Then my uncle smiled, and I saw those teeth again. I licked down to the sugar cone and took my first bite. "I do have something. It's a horse laxative. But you only can use the tiniest bit— a man is not a horse—otherwise, you'll kill him."

My father lit up.

Uncle Sam slipped him a brown bottle with a rubber dropper, just as my mother came out of the ladies' room in a black velvet hat with a red bird on top. A fresh smear of lipstick was across her face. My father palmed the bottle into his trouser pocket.

"Careful, Buddy," my uncle said again and then, "Sylvia, you look beautiful." My mother flashed her dark eyes.

Another red traffic light. My father pulled out the ashtray and balanced his cigar on the edge. Then he continued, "When that lousy man came in again and ordered his third drink, I turned my back to the bar to pour it. I touched, just touched, the rim of the glass with that golden liquid in the dropper. I slapped that glass on the bar, 'This one's on me,' and I leaned back and watched."

The light changed to green. The car behind us honked its horn. My father took his foot off the brake and ever so slightly applied the gas. Then he continued, "The man bolted down the drink, and faster than his mind could think," he smiled at the rhyme and at the memory, "the laxative ran through his body. He was about to say, 'Where's the bathroom?' but he'd already done his business. And I just nodded congenial-like. He turned red and ran out the door."

"What if you killed him?" I asked.

"I didn't kill that tough bastard, but I never saw him again."

"What was his name?"

My father turned and looked at me suspiciously. "You're not going to write about it?"

"No, of course not."

"Ahh, what the hell. He deserved it."

We parked the car and were standing on the concrete step in front of my room. He grabbed me by the shoulders. "I love you." He paused. "I love you—I *really* love you." These weren't just words family members said to one another. A connection was being made. Here we were together, this one lifetime, me and him. He loved his daughter.

He started to take off the ruby ring. "It's your inheritance. Take it now."

I shook my head and put my hand on his wrist.

"You wear it," I said.

I never wanted him to die.

THE NEXT MORNING I was sitting at gate thirty-four, Delta, waiting to board the plane at five fifteen. Was that my father in the empty distance down at gate twenty-three, coming toward me walking his lopsided walk, heavy to the right, in a blue T-shirt and khaki Bermudas, carrying a bag?

"Gee, I was afraid you'd already left. I grabbed some fruit. You'll get hungry." He reached out the sack and was pleased.

I looked in—a brown banana and two apples. "I got them from the kitchen." I looked up at him. His smile hardly revealed his small teeth, darkened and close together in front.

At least four or five of his back teeth had been pulled. When the dentist told him how much a root canal would cost and then the capping, he said straight out, "Pull."

The dentist stuttered, tried to explain the necessity of—

My father cut him off. "You've got to be kidding—twelve hundred dollars! I don't like my teeth that much." He opened his mouth wide. "Go ahead. Do as I say, pull."

I thanked him for the fruit. "I do get hungry on these long flights."

He nodded, satisfied that he knew to do the right thing. "Well, I won't hang around. I got things to do." At eighty-two he no longer played golf or tennis. He mostly spent his days in front of the TV with the shades pulled against the southern sun.

"Sure," I said.

He raised his big paw, turned, and I watched him walk away. From the back I saw his right hand raised to his face. He was wiping away tears.

Time felt convoluted. I'd tumbled from youth, and my father had shot through to old age.

PART 2

*I can write a beautiful piece about the red rock
desert, but if I don't talk about the fact that if you just
switch your eyes a little bit to the left you'll see the
results of oil and gas leases . . . that doesn't quite
seem honest. And a hundred years from now,
I don't want someone to say, where was she?
Why didn't she tell us the truth?*

—TERRY TEMPEST WILLIAMS

Te-shan asked the old tea-cake woman, "Who is your teacher? Where did you learn this?"

She pointed to a monastery a half mile away.

Te-shan visited Lung-t'an and questioned him far into the night. Finally when it was very late, Lung-t'an said, "Why don't you go and rest now?"

Te-shan thanked him and opened the door. "It's dark outside. I can't see."

Lung-t'an lit a candle for him, but just as Te-shan turned and reached out to take it, Lung-t'an blew it out.

At that moment Te-shan had a great enlightenment. Full of gratitude, he bowed deeply to Lung-t'an.

The next day Lung-t'an praised Te-shan to the assembly of monks. Te-shan brought his books and commentaries in front of the building and lit them on fire, saying, "These notes are nothing, like placing a hair in vast space."

Then bowing again to his teacher, he left.

THE THURSDAY NIGHT I flew into Minneapolis and saw Katagiri Roshi's body laid out in the zendo (meditation hall), dead eighteen hours from a cancer he fought for

over a year, was also the night I had slipped the original
letter to my father into the blue mailbox. I flipped the
stone-cold metal lid and heard the long white envelope
hit the bottom. I was standing across the street from
Zen Center at the edge of Lake Calhoun, where the
solid ice was only beginning to break up. Even though it
was past midnight, thick gray clouds hovered low in
the sky. I'd carried that letter in my purse for over a
month. The immense disappointment at seeing Roshi
dead shocked me into finally sending it. Now I would
lose both fathers.

But mail is slower than we think. The date was March
first. It was probably picked up on March second. My
father did not receive it until the morning of March seventh, his birthday. I never planned it that way. I didn't
think about it. My father, ordinarily not a thoughtful
man, did. "My birthday? Why would you do that?" My
father liked his birthday and wanted to enjoy his day.

It was incomprehensible that I would never see my
beloved teacher again. My father was the only one I knew
who had sneered at death's bleak face as he fought in the
righteous war that marked his life. Of everyone I knew,
he alone did not seem afraid of the great darkness. "Nat,
you're here and then you're not. Don't worry about it. It's
not a big deal," he told me as he placed a pile of army
photos on my lap. "The Japanese, you have to give it to
'em. They could really fight. Tough, good soldiers." Then

he held up a black-and-white. "Here's your handsome daddy overseas."

Roshi also fought as a young man in World War II. He told a story about not wanting to kill and shooting in the air above enemy heads. I told that to my father. "What a lot of malarkey," my father sneered. "You don't believe that, do you? You're in battle, you fight."

My father met my teacher only once, about a year after I had married. We had just bought the lower half of a duplex on a leafy tree–lined one-way street six blocks from Zen Center in Minneapolis. I was in my early thirties, and my parents drove out for a week in July. They were still young, in their early sixties.

In the middle of one afternoon when no one was around, we slipped off our shoes and stepped onto the high-shined wooden floor of the zendo. My parents peered at bare white walls, black cushions, and a simple wooden altar with a statue and some flowers.

I heard the door in the hall open. "I bet that's Roshi."

My father's eyes grew wide. His face swung to the large screened window, and for a moment I thought he was going to crash through in a grand escape. Pearls of sweat formed on his upper lip.

Roshi turned the corner. They stood across the room from each other. The meeting was brief. They never shook hands. My father was subdued, withdrawn, and Roshi too wasn't his usual animated self.

I remember thinking, my father has become shy in front of a Zen master—finally someone tamed him.

I got it all wrong. He didn't give a shit about that. He had just encountered the enemy face-to-face. After Roshi exited, he hissed, "I fought them, and now you're studying with them."

"IF THIS WERE YOUR last moment on earth," Roshi cut the silence with these words late at night, "how would you sit?" We were waiting for the bell to ring. It was the end of a weeklong retreat. Our knees and backs ached. The candle flame hissed; the smell of incense from Eiheiji monastery (the Japanese training center for Soto Zen), shipped in cartons to Minnesota, soaked our clothes.

"You've got to be kidding. Just ring the damn bell," was the only thought that raced through my head.

On other occasions when he asked similar questions, my mind froze. Me, die? Not possible.

Death was something aesthetic, artistic; it had to do with the grand words "forever," "eternity," "emptiness." I never had known anyone who had died before. It was merely a practice point: everything is impermanent. Sure, sure. But really it was inconceivable that my body would not be my body. I was lean, young, and everything worked. I had a name, an identity: Natalie Goldberg.

What a shock it was for me to see my great teacher's stiff body. This was for real? The man I had studied with for twelve years was gone? Stars, moon, hope stopped.

Ocean waves and ants froze. Even rocks would not grow. This truth I could not bear.

Wait a minute! Wasn't he the one who urged me to create writing as a Zen practice? Didn't I do that—and wrote a book about it? Vice presidents of insurance agencies, factory workers in Nebraska, quarry diggers in Missouri, lawyers, doctors, housewives, all with secret, tender hearts yearning to step forward and speak, were sending me fan letters. After eons of fear from stiff school curriculums, I gave them the tools to write. I was doing my part for Zen in this country, saving sentient Americans all over the place.

And, Roshi, I did it for you. I couldn't have done it alone. You were always at my back. And now you're dead? Impossible. I'm out there alone? My breath caught. This can't be. I won't take death seriously—you must be someplace. I'll come find you. Heaven? Hell? Give me a minute. I'll figure it out. I'm coming for you.

My panic was real. I only had one tool: I immediately dove into creating another book. Writing was all-powerful for me. I would keep him alive this way. I would write about the cuffed jeans he wore when he worked on the land, the wild smile that showed the bottom of his teeth, his thick arms, how he fell off the zafu (meditation cushion) laughing when I'd tell him a marriage problem. I'd tug at his priest robe. "Very funny, yes. Now help me."

For the two years I wrote, he stayed vividly alive. He was with me.

Although I didn't speak to my father for a long time after the trauma of sending the letter, I still considered myself a lucky woman, as I leaned over my notebook writing the book about Roshi. Maybe my childhood wasn't so great, but look who I had found, this man from another country. I could step out of my own skin and be free. I began the first pages explaining in detail my lost suburban childhood and then on page one hundred, bingo! I met Roshi.

I was guided by three great teachings I received from him:

Continue Under All Circumstances
Don't Be Tossed Away—Don't Let Anything Stop You
Make Positive Effort for the Good

The last one Roshi told me when I was divorcing and couldn't get out of bed.

"If nothing else, get up and brush your teeth." He paused. "I can never get up when the alarm goes off. Nevertheless," he nodded, "I get up."

Once in the early days I was perplexed about trees. I asked at the end of a lecture, "Roshi, do the elms suffer?"

He answered.

"What? Could you tell me again? Do they really suffer?" I couldn't take it in.

He shot back his reply.

It pinged off my forehead and did not penetrate. I was

caught in thinking mind, too busy trying to understand everything.

But my confusion had drive. I raised my hand a third time. "Roshi, just once more. I don't get it. I mean do trees *really* suffer."

He looked straight at me. "Shut up."

That went in.

The amazing thing was I did not take it personally. He was directly commanding my monkey mind to stop. I'd already been studying with him for a while. Those two words were a relief. Dead end. Quit. I rested back into my sitting position and felt my breath go in and out at my nose. The thought about trees that evening stopped grabbing me by the throat.

With him extraneous things were cut away. My life force stepped forward. After a sleepy childhood I was seen and understood. Glory! Glory! I had found a great teacher in the deep north of this country. Maybe that had been the purpose of my short marriage: to bring me here. Both Roshi and I did not belong in Minnesota, yet we had found each other.

I positioned Roshi in the deep gash I had in my heart. He took the place of loneliness and desolation, and with him as a bolster I felt whole. But the deal was he had to stay alive, continue existing, for this configuration to work.

I sat by the hot oven as his body was cremated. All that was left was ashes. I took two years to finish the book about him and then I really faced the end: Where was he?

I traveled to Czechoslovakia with my friend Carol to celebrate the book's completion, but there was no rejoicing. That was when it all came home: I was deeply, deeply alone. No Zen teacher, and no blood father either.

We were in Karlovy Vary, a beautiful resort town, a hiatus in all the destructive history of Czechoslovakia.

Carol wrote down the most precise directions for me to meet her at the bus station to ride back to Prague at the end of the day: walk down the main avenue, cross the railroad tracks, make a left, a right . . . She could tell I was preoccupied, and she didn't want me to miss the bus back.

"Uh-huh," I nodded and stuck the paper slip in my pocket.

Large chestnut trees lined the park; the leaves' broad edges had turned yellow, red, and orange. I bent to pocket three large mahogany nuts for a friend in New Mexico.

"Karlovy Vary," I repeated like a chant. Writers have come to you. What is it you have?

Goethe was an old man when he visited with a very young consort. It would have been scandalous, but it was Goethe—he was a great literary figure—and it was Europe. Worse things had happened. Rilke was here for refuge and relaxation. I liked this place. I felt connected.

Shadows were lengthening. I finished the pistachio ice cream I ate out of a silver dish, put some coins on the small round marble table, and pulled the crumpled note from my pocket.

I reread the directions. I'd wandered far from the place that Carol's directions began from. No matter. I pursed my lips and set out. Travel imbued me with a poignancy; I felt a grand weight for each step, brick, storefront. None of this will last forever. Each moment vividly presented itself. I felt a lump in my throat, a thump in my heart, the pulse of my blood. Now and now and now. I was back in the romance of eternity.

I realized I hadn't thought of Roshi in days. What a relief! I congratulated myself. Then at the edge of a line of shops, I turned at a souvenir cart—I don't know how to say this—in the twilight I saw a tree. At least ten feet tall, buoyant, arms extended, leaves bright green. But the tree was nameless. I dropped my suitcase. How was it possible? I lowered myself onto a bench. People rushed by.

"So this is where you've ended up? While they carry your ashes to Tassajara in Carmel Valley and Hokyoji in Minnesota and Taisoin in Japan, you have escaped into a tree."

I sat contentedly in the growing dark. I never wanted to leave.

Suddenly, my happiness cracked. I remembered: the bus! Carol! Czechoslovakia! My God! I ripped myself away from the ten thousand leaves and tore through the cobbled streets toward the narrow highway where the station was. I flew into the ticket man's chest as he tried to signal with his hands: no more buses.

"No, no, no," I screamed, dropping any pretense of being human.

A cry from the back of a receding bus, a screech of brakes, and then my name yelled out in the dark. I grabbed my bag and ran. Carol beckoned through the window with her arms.

I flung myself into the backseat. We tilted as the vehicle swung around a curve and banged us on the hard wooden seats.

"We were late in leaving," she explained.

I looked at her and nodded. I leaned my cheek against the cold glass as we rolled through the mysterious countryside. "Karlovy Vary, Karlovy Vary," I whispered. Goethe found love. Rilke, poetry. And what do you know? I found Roshi.

But that elation did not last.

Soon after our visit to Prague, the book came out, and my publisher arranged a tour. For my first two books, I hadn't gone on one. I'd heard hard stories from other writers about late planes, missed interviews, being stranded in the wrong city, getting a cold and sounding like a foghorn, losing bearings and referring on radio to the wrong town, the one you were in last week. But for Roshi I would do it. Even if I no longer had him, he should be shared with others. Maybe they would benefit as I had. Maybe too I wouldn't feel so alone in my grief. I kept wondering who I would write for now. What great purpose would again spring me into action?

In the back of cabs going to airports from Minneapolis, St. Louis, Washington, D.C., Boston, Milwaukee, my body collapsed with exhaustion. I can't do this anymore—and then, miraculously, I experienced energy fill me from some source outside myself. I was so pleased, I did not question it.

In Seattle, my tenth city, the escort, who took me to radio stations, bookstore readings, the hotel, was particularly lovely. "You seem to be doing okay." She eyed me cautiously in the passenger seat as she drove me to the airport. "The last one I drove around two days ago caught a stomach flu and sat with a bucket between her legs." She turned a corner. "If you know even one person in the audience, it seems to help and make a difference. You don't feel so dislocated."

Yes, it was true. I was lucky. I did know people everywhere I went. But Portland, Oregon, was next. I'd never been there. I didn't know a single soul. I'd held out well, but I was worn out.

The short plane ride from Seattle to Portland left at five in the morning. The publisher wanted to make sure nothing would keep me from a newspaper interview at ten. At six thirty the new escort, Deirdre, was waiting at the gate. She began talking as soon as she saw me. "I've made a decision this year to tell every author I work with about political issues I think are important."

"Please don't," I said silently as I looked out the window. A terrible headache was converging over my eyebrows. We were stuck in traffic. She launched into a tirade about lesbians, then one on abortion, and another on the evils of taxes.

I sunk deeper in the car seat. I had no energy to assert my opinion.

"You have a noon brown bag at Cat Bird Seat Bookstore downtown. The idea is that people can come hear you during their lunch hour. But no one ever comes. You'll be lucky if you sell one book. We can be late." Deirdre pressed both hands against the top of the steering wheel. "Would you like to stop at the hotel first?"

"Yes!" I almost jumped through the roof of the car. A moment to get away. Yes, yes, yes.

When we pulled up in front of the bookstore, it was jammed. I had so thoroughly believed Deirdre that I turned to the manager, who rushed at me, and asked, "Did you have a speaker today?"

"Yes—you're late." She grabbed my elbow and hurried me up front.

I looked out on a crowded room; most people were sitting on the carpeted floor. I read a short piece about how I first met Roshi, then opened it up for discussion.

The audience's questions surprised me. "How many of you are Zen students?" I asked.

No one raised their hand. "In no other group all over the country did anyone ask me anything about Buddhism, even though this," I held up my book, "is about my twelve-year relationship with a Zen teacher. But your comments are detailed and technical about aspects of sitting. No center here either?"

People shook their heads.

"Hmmm." I looked at the clock above their heads. "I better sign books. Lunch hour is almost up."

A long line formed out the door. I settled into a seat at the table. This would take a while. I was lonely, and I was tired. I knew no one in this town, but I tried my best.

I signed a new book on the title page.

I signed the next woman's. She had an old copy of my first.

The third woman held a pile of three book-club copies, two used and one new. "You've got them all," I teased her.

She was in a flutter and wanted certain pages signed in each one.

Ahh, I'll take a little rest while she opens them. I had no other thought in my head. I leaned back in the chair and glanced over to the checkout—there he was! leaning his elbows on the counter. The arms of his koromo (priest robe) were tied back like they were when he swept the walk, raked under the elm out back of the zendo. Every time the cash register rang, the drawer snapped open and he broke into laughter, rubbing his shaved head with his hand. Many people were buying this book about him. Another purchase, another ring. The change tray flew out, and again he laughed, this time with his chin in his chunky muscled hand. I don't think it was the book sales that delighted him. It was the silly mechanism of the spirited register that caused his glee, a bonus he hadn't expected. He was here to pay a visit to his former student, so she wouldn't be lost in an unknown town.

And his old student drank in his presence for as long as she could—one very good long moment.

The woman cleared her throat to get my attention. Her opened books were piled in front of me on the table. She had found her places.

"Oh, yes," I said and dragged my attention away from Roshi.

I picked up my pen and wrote my name in the top one. I dated it: the month, the year, the day, even the time. I wrote "in Portland, Oregon" with great assurance. Then I drew a small heart next to the state name to stamp the secret in place, that he was here.

The last time I saw Roshi alive he was lying in bed in his apartment above the zendo in Minneapolis, Minnesota. His wife was reading him a letter from a former student. He'd received a lot of mail. In his last months he had been dismayed that he hadn't done very much in America, but the messages overwhelmingly thanked him for how he'd changed lives. He was listening attentively to the words his wife read. I didn't want to interrupt, so I stayed briefly. I was returning to New Mexico the next day. Just as I opened the door to leave, he called out, "I'll see you again."

"Sure," I agreed, but I knew he was dying. In all our interactions he was careful to make teaching points. He was never casual with me. Maybe he was worn out from making any point. This one time perhaps he just threw out an American colloquialism, "See ya again." Or could he have been in denial about his sickness?

I leaned over past the next person, who was handing me a book, but Roshi was gone. I knew, though, with certainty that he'd kept his promise. But this was no magic, no white knight who came to save me. Great effort, not my individual will, had harnessed these forces, allowed this moment to coalesce. He manifested in support not of me but of the dharma, of the sharing of teachings.

Deirdre came to get me. I gave her a big grin. It was then that I fell into a trap: thinking the visit was personal and maybe if I kept making effort, he'd keep returning, death be damned. But in a moment I let go, and as we walked to the Chevy, I only felt happy: I got to see him again.

A BOOK IS A PUBLIC THING. I became known as Katagiri Roshi's student. I felt lucky to have known him, but my heart was tied to a dead man. I couldn't let go, and I couldn't go on.

The third year after his death was the worst in my life. Through the book people were loving Roshi, but there was no one to love, only an image made of words. I wrote those words, and while I was writing I was oblivious to the finality of his passing. But in that third year, I felt the strong winds of New Mexico blow through the hole in my chest.

Our process had been cut short. In a healthy teacher-student relationship, the teacher calls out of the student a large vision of what is possible. I finally dared to feel the great true dream I had inside. I projected it onto this person who was my teacher. This projection was part of spiritual development. It allowed me to discover the largeness of my own psyche, but it wasn't based on some illusion. Roshi possessed many of these projected qualities, but each student was individual. When I asked other practitioners what impressed them about Katagiri Roshi, the reported qualities were different for each person. One woman in Santa Cruz admired his unerring self-confidence. When she visited me in New Mexico she stood up and imitated his physical stance. She said that even when no one understood his English and we weren't sure of the Buddhist concepts he discussed, he bowed in front of the altar and walked out after his lecture as though all time and the universe were backing him.

I'd never even taken note of that. What I loved was his enthusiasm, his ability to be in the moment and not judge and categorize me. He had a great sense of humor. I admired his dedication to practice and to all beings and his willingness to tell me the truth, with no effort to sweeten it.

Eventually, as the teacher-student relationship matures, the student manifests these qualities herself and learns to stand on her own two feet. The projections are reclaimed. What we saw in him is also inside us. We close the gap between who we think the teacher is and who we think we are not. We become whole.

Roshi died before this process was finished. I felt like a green fruit. I still needed the sun, the rain, the nutrients of the tree. Instead, the great oak withered; I dangled for a while and then fell to the ground, very undernourished.

How many of us get to live out the full maturation process? Our modern lives are built on speed. We move fast, never settle. Most of us grab what we can, a little from here, then there. For twelve years I had one source. I should have been satisfied. He gave me everything. I knew that when I saw his dead body, but how to live it inside myself?

This projection process also can get more complicated if we haven't individuated from our original parents. Then we present to the teacher those undeveloped parts too. Here the teacher needs to be savvy, alert, and committed in order to avoid taking advantage of vulnerable students. I have read about Zen ancestors who practiced with their teachers for forty years in a single monastery, and I understand why. There would be no half-baked characters in those ancient lineages.

But, oddly enough, Te-shan only had that one meeting with Lung-t'an, and he woke up. Of course, he was a serious scholar of the dharma for a long time. Who is to say scholarly pursuits—studying books intently and writing commentary—don't prepare the mind as well as sweeping bamboo-lined walkways, sitting long hours, or preparing monastery meals?

Zen training is physical. But what isn't physical while we have a body on this earth? Sitting bent over books, our eyes following a line of print, is physical too. So that when Te-shan had that single evening in Lung-t'an's room, he was already very ripe. Lung-t'an merely had to push him off the tree, and Te-shan was prepared to fall into the tremendous empty dark with no clinging.

Te-shan was shown true darkness when Lung-t'an blew out the light; he held at last a dharma candle to guide his way, but he still had a lot of maturation ahead of him. Don't forget the next morning he made that grandiose gesture of burning his books in front of the assembly of monks. He was still acting out, choosing this and leaving that. He was not yet able to honor his whole journey, to respect everything that brought him to this moment. Te-shan still envisioned things in dualistic terms: now only direct insight mattered; books needed to be destroyed. He didn't see that all those years of study had created a foundation that supported his awakening with Lung-t'an. Originally he traveled from the north with his sutras on his back to enlighten the southern barbarians. Here he was doing a complete reversal, torching his past and revering his present experience. Someday he would embrace the north and the south, unify all of China in his heart, and attain a peaceful mind. But he was not there yet. We see him engaged in drama, presenting a flaming pageant in front of the other monks.

His life had not yet settled and become calm.

After he left Lung-t'an, he wandered for a long time, looking to be tested and sharpened. He already had left his place in northern China to wander among what he thought were the southern barbarians. He might be the precursor to our fractured American way of searching for peace.

How can anyone survive if the way is so splintered? What we learn is it's all whole, been whole all along. It is our perception that is broken and that creates a shattered world. But each of us has to discover this in our own lives. That is what is so hard.

"I wish you'd gotten to meet him," I'd tell writing students.

"We are," they'd say, meaning they did through knowing me.

I scoffed. "You don't know what you're talking about."

At a party in San Francisco, Ed Brown, a longtime Zen practitioner and author of many books, pulled me over. "Nat, I have another story about Katagiri for you to steal."

I laughed. I'd asked his permission and acknowledged him with the last one I used. I put my arm around him. "Sure, Ed, give it to me. I'd love to steal from you again."

He began, "I'd been practicing for twenty years when the thought suddenly came to me, 'Ed, maybe you can just hear what your heart is saying. You can be quiet and pay attention to yourself.' It was a big moment of relief for me. Tears filled my eyes."

He showed me with his fingers how they fell down his cheeks. "I'd tried so hard all my life. Made such effort, lived in a monastery since I was young. And now this. Could it be that simple?

"The next day I had an interview with Katagiri. I asked him, 'Do you think it's okay to just listen to yourself?'

"He looked down, then he looked up. 'Ed, I tried very hard to practice Dogen's Zen. After twenty years I realized there was no Dogen's Zen.'"

Dogen was a strict patriarch from thirteenth-century Japan. We chanted his words each morning. He was a yardstick by which we measured ourselves.

I felt my legs buckle. I reached out for the back of a chair. Just us. No heaven Zen in some Asian sky out there.

I put my hand on Ed's shoulder. "Ed, I vow to once again misappropriate your story." He nodded, satisfied.

I was reminded how simple, sincere, earnest Roshi was. I was happy, and then it ignited my anger. I was mad he died. I had found the perfect teacher.

I tried practicing other places. I did two fall practice periods at Green Gulch, part of the San Francisco Zen

Center. While I was there, an old student told me about the early years at the Zen monastery in Carmel Valley.

Tassajara was in a narrow valley. The sun didn't reach it until late morning, rising over an eastern mountain, and it dropped early behind the slope of a western one. The practice was difficult, and the days and nights were frigid and damp. But American students of the late sixties were fervent about this path to liberate their lives. One particular winter retreat that lasted for a hundred days was being led by Katagiri, fresh from Japan.

One young zealous woman, a fierce practitioner, a bit Zen crazed, was having a hard time. She was full of resistance when the four o'clock wake-up bell rang on the fifth day of Rohatsu sesshin, an intense week that honored Buddha's enlightenment and signaled almost the finish of the long retreat. Practice that day would again be from four thirty in the morning until ten at night with few breaks except for short walking meditations (kinhin) and an hour work period after lunch. It was her turn that morning to carry the kyosaku, that long narrow board administered in the zendo to sleepy students' shoulders. Her hands were frozen and her bare feet were ice on the cold wooden floor when she got there. She picked up the wake-up stick and passed quietly by the altar to do the ritual bow to Katagiri, the head teacher, who was facing into the room. The flame on the candle was strong. The incense wafted through the air. The practitioners were settled onto their cushions, facing out toward the wall.

A thought inflamed her just as she was about to bow in front of Katagiri: it's easy for him. He's Asian. He's been doing this all his life. It's second nature. His body just folds into position.

Though it is a rule of retreat that people do not look at each other, in order to limit social interaction and provide psychic space for going deeply within, at this moment she glanced up at Roshi. She was stunned to see pearls of sweat forming on his upper lip. Only one reason he could have been perspiring in this frozen zendo: great effort. It wasn't any easier for him than anyone else. Was she ever wrong in her assumptions. She had gotten close enough to see what no one was supposed to see. All her rage and stereotyping crumbled.

My heart jumped. I imagined the small hard dark hairs above his lip—he did not shave for the whole week during sesshins. I recalled the shadow building on his cheeks and shaved head as the days went on, how he bowed with his hands pressed together in front of him, elbows out, and shoulders erect. His small beautiful foot as he placed a step on the floor during kinhin. Though retreats were austere, singular, solitary, there was also a rare intimacy that was shared in silence and practice together.

Just two weeks before the end of the second Green Gulch retreat, in December 1995, almost six years after Katagiri Roshi had died, in a stunning moment in the zendo that shot through me like a hot steel bolt, I realized this regimented practice no longer fit me. The known world blanked out, and I was lost in the moving weight of a waterfall. For me, the structure *was* Katagiri Roshi. I learned it all from him. If I stepped out of it, I'd lose my great teacher. I knew how to wake at four o'clock in the morning, to sit still for forty-minute periods, to eat with three bowls in concentration—it was over, other parts of me needed care. Structure had saved my life, given me a foundation, and now it was cracking. It was a big opening, but I wasn't up to it.

After the practice period I stayed at a friend's south of San Francisco, recuperating from one of those terrible winter flus that flatten a person for three weeks. Below the surface of sneezing and blowing my nose, in the place I could not touch, I feared I would lose Roshi. I wanted so bad to keep him alive, and I thought the fierce structure of Zen was the way. The conflict of holding on and needing to let go made me sick and gloomy, as I lay in bed.

My friend handed me a cup of hot tea. Right before she went to the movies, she changed the bedsheets, while I took a shower. As I slipped into the fresh linen, the phone rang. I almost didn't answer. Let the machine pick it up. It couldn't be for me. Hardly anyone knew I was there. The phone was on a small table on the left side of the bed. The humidifier was whistling as I lifted the mouthpiece and in a nasal voice whispered, "Hello."

"Natalie, it's Peter." He had been at the Minnesota Zen Center, but we rarely had reason to speak in the last two or three years. How did he find me here? "I have something to tell you."

My eyes were swollen, and my ears hurt. "What?" I innocently asked.

"Roshi's priests were in a teachers' meeting, and it came out that Roshi had slept with a student."

My nose was running. Where were my tissues? "Huh?" I asked. I must have misheard.

"A student had lodged a complaint about a sexual indiscretion with one of Roshi's dharma heirs, and Eleanor got all heated up and suddenly blurted out, 'I don't know what the big deal is. Roshi and I had a reationship for a year and—' Then she abruptly stopped and threw her hand over her mouth. She realized what she'd said. We all turned to her—no one cared about the other problem anymore. We just stared at her."

I pictured the whole thing in my groggy head. I knew all the dharma heirs well, the twelve priests Roshi had given transmission to, added their names to his ancient lineage just before he died. We'd all practiced together. He said no one was ready to take over, but he hoped to avoid his heirs becoming competitive and political, and maybe in time someone would ripen and step forward. I wanted that transmission too, but couldn't get it. I wasn't a priest. I could see them at the meeting, sitting in a circle at the old center, a house on Lake Calhoun. Eleanor's freckled face came on in a high flush, while the other faces went white and numb. Their suddenly weighted heads bent over like ripe sunflowers, too heavy for their necks, as they stared at her in a boundless silence.

I too was silent. I didn't know what to say, so Peter continued.

At the same time almost to the day that we found out about Eleanor, another dharma teacher out in California discovered that a Zen student in Detroit had acted as a confidante for Roshi and had helped him out with at least one other woman Zen student in that city.

I put my hand to my forehead. Was I running a fever? I couldn't possibly be hearing what I was hearing.

The actions were so discreet it took six years after my teacher's death for them to be unveiled. Then the secret, unviewed for so long, suddenly unreeled, exposing itself across the country.

A splitting headache over my left eye was coming on as Peter continued to speak. It must be this flu. I shook my head to push the ache away.

Peter was profoundly disturbed, but I could come up with only one dumb comment. "Well, at least he was getting some all those years." Then I scrunched deeper under the covers. I felt unsafe.

I thanked him for calling. I placed the phone down as if it were a bad-smelling fish. I wanted it out of my hand.

For two hours I blanked out and denied Peter had called. I just lay in bed and stared up at the ceiling. I even forgot I ever studied Zen, that I crossed my legs in a sitting meditation position, that I knew where Japan or Minneapolis was on the globe of the world.

When my friend returned, I asked her about the movie. A man was in love with a woman, but she wasn't sure about him. He drove a Mercedes and she liked that, but something about him scared her. My friend loved to tell every detail. Usually I interrupted her and said I didn't want a blow-by-blow synopsis. Only kids do that: "This happened, then this." I usually told her to give me the texture, analysis, conflict point—we were old Jewish friends and could be blunt with each other—but this evening I nodded my head as one detail after another, one scene and then another unrolled. I was the thirteenth sunflower in Katagiri's lineage, nodding my heavy head. Uh-huh, uh-huh, uh-huh.

At first my friend was delighted—I was listening to her rehash—but then she stopped. "What's wrong?"

"Roshi had relations with one of his female students." My feeble body couldn't hold back the movement of an ancient glacier, an old crystallized story. "I'm exhausted. I'm going to sleep."

This was the same thing that happened with my father, different but the same. My heart loved them both, but now I held raw knowledge—betrayal dripped off my gripped hand.

Five days later, I flew home from California. Taos seemed empty—not the empty I loved there in winter, the sky a deeper blue, the distant mountaintops crested with snow, the bite of a dry, clear cold, and the smell of cedar and piñon fires—but just vacant. I tried hard to keep my balance after this landslide of new knowledge. I rationalized he was a Japanese man. The attitude of Japanese men about relationships with women was different. Maybe it was acceptable to be married and have mistresses or affairs. I asked myself a pragmatic question: What power did you project on Roshi that you can now claim for yourself? That's the one all my friends asked. That's all I had to do, they said: take back the power. I tried to grab hold with that one, but I knew it did not come close to the hurricane I felt inside.

I MET ROSHI WHEN I WAS THIRTY. Because of his support, I wrote books. His great betrayal before this had been that he died, left me too early. I had made him perfect, so I could feel safe to go deep and let my life bloom. Because of my family abuse, I was driven to get what I had longed for in my family—clear recognition with no sexual overtones—and with Roshi nothing was going to interrupt it.

My father was sleeping on a couch at his in-laws' apartment in Brooklyn and my mother was in a daze, unconscious on drugs, when I zoomed out between her legs into the abundant world. No one was there to welcome me. I was raised in the somnambulant suburbs. When I met Roshi, I recognized life in this shining man before me. I needed to be reflected in another. By the time

I encountered him, I was ravenous. Unknowingly, Roshi became my mother, my father, my Zen master.

While sex scandals broke up other Zen and Eastern religious communities, I felt safe with my teacher. Everyone knew he was clean. Robert Aitken, an American Zen teacher in Hawaii, had been known to repeat, "Thank god for Katagiri Roshi—he's the one who gives us hope." My childhood had been preoccupied with protecting myself from my father. In Zen, with its strict structure, I felt free to explore whole parts of myself without keeping my guard up.

I felt gratitude toward Peter for calling, directly, before the information was covered up or reduced to some half rumor, swallowed into a secret silence, people turning their backs if someone poked around. I'd seen it happen before in other communities. Nevertheless, the information was devastating. I could not find an easy conclusion. I no longer had any ground below me. Every time I tried to find my feet, the foothold crumbled.

I sat at my desk on the mesa one afternoon. I needed to get back to the novel I was working on, I told myself. The pen hovered above the page, but I looked blankly ahead out the window, not seeing the newly planted piñons. Instead, I was remembering the first floor of a duplex on Emerson Avenue near Zen Center. I was newly married. We were having a potluck in our living room. Even our simple home had a built-in oak commode with leaded-glass windows. The gray carpet was thin and rubbed raw in spots. All the Zen students were there that early summer evening. My first book of poetry had just been published by a small Minnesota press, and there was some publicity in the local uptown neighborhood newspaper.

Roshi, who had a can of beer in his hand, came up to me. He beamed with his shaved head. We were about the same height. He was in his early fifties, twenty years older than me, full of vitality, wearing jeans and a white T-shirt.

"I saw your photograph in the newspaper," he spoke in a broken English, but by this time I understood him easily.

I nodded and smiled. I was proud and happy he had noticed my accomplishment.

"You are very beautiful."

I did not expect this. "Thank you," I said cheerily, covering up my confusion, acting extra innocent, young, girlish. Roshi had never talked this way before.

He saw that I was not recording the hidden significance of my beauty. He repeated again with more intensity and emphasis, "No, you are very beautiful. Do you know that?" His words were now directly pointed at me, obviously full of innuendo.

I was confused, something was terribly askew—we were in another dimension.

Yet I was not a complete fool—I knew what he was getting at—but this couldn't be Roshi. This man was too creepy. I blithely thanked him for his compliment, walked away, and stayed away the rest of the evening.

It must have been the beer. Roshi's wife had been out of town, his two sons off somewhere. I forgot the incident, and I never mentioned it to anyone, not even my husband. I continued to study with him for the next ten years. Luckily, it never came up again.

The sound of ravens' wings flapping over my house heading east brought me back to the huge stillness on the mesa. But right then nothing could hold me. My thoughts pressed on.

I didn't realize it, but after that encounter I was unconsciously more diligent about our interactions. I kept my relationship with Roshi narrow, assiduously defined the parameters of our interactions—practice periods, work periods, retreats, formal settings. I stayed one-pointed in my encounters with him. No after-dinner meetings, being a board member, driving him places alone. After a lifetime of childhood training fending off my father, I wasn't going to be threatened by that one time. I had it all under lock and key.

Then I remembered hearing that a similar incident happened to another student the same weekend. Could this experience have been repeated: Roshi threw out a hook, and if there was no bite, he'd let go? I grimaced as I sat all alone in my studio next to the zendo I had built in his honor.

Two days after I returned home I received a call from a friend living in Australia. She said back when she was practicing with Roshi, she spoke to him about her marriage troubles. "What he advised stunned me—he told me I should have an affair! At the time I just thought, 'I don't understand this Zen.' I wonder now what he was really getting at."

My teeth ground together. This was hard to hear. But what were we doing going to him about relationship, work, probably even car problems? We were mixed up about Roshi's position. We wanted to learn Zen from him, but wasn't Zen in everything? Because his role was never clarified, we filled the vacuum with our expectations. Wouldn't he also know about plumbing? There was nothing a Zen master didn't understand.

This probably was not a problem in Japan, where a priest's position was clearly defined and built into society's fabric. But here in the United States, where Zen perfume, Zen beds, Zen beads were sold, we could project wildly on Zen's true purpose.

At first Roshi must have been surprised by what we brought to him. Then curiosity might have taken over. He was a man sincerely motivated by wanting to help human beings. But somewhere along the line, I guess, he became confused by the female abundance he found at American centers, so different from Japanese monasteries.

The last of December moved farther into darkness, the evenings coming early, the sun rising late over the mountain. I sat by myself through the shadowy days, but I could not get a handle on this new information. I didn't talk about it with New Mexico friends. They didn't know Roshi, and it was too easy to hear "Roshi slept with a student" and just write him off. I still felt protective.

In the middle of January I conducted a weeklong writing workshop at the Mabel Dodge Luhan House in Taos. Sixty people from all over the country attended. I taught well and was certain I had a handle on all this Roshi stuff. Then on Wednesday morning, standing up in front of the class, I didn't feel well. After class I noticed blisters had formed along my left hip. They burned and itched badly enough that during lunch I called my friend Carol, the dermatologist, in Minnesota. I described the symptoms.

"What's going on?" I had to be with my students in fifteen minutes.

"It sounds like shingles."

"Not again!" I had had an outbreak for the first and only time six years earlier when Roshi died.

"But that time was on the left side of your face?" Carol's a good friend and remembers these details. "Nat, further outbreaks, I'm almost certain, always happen in the same place. I've never heard of it breaking out in another place, but it definitely sounds like shingles."

She told me at this point there was nothing much I could do, but after the workshop I should have a dermatologist look at it anyway.

I moaned. With no dermatologist in Taos, I'd have to drive an hour and a half to Santa Fe.

"Have you been under a lot of stress lately?" Carol asked.

We hung up. My mind began to unravel. The old world, the one I constructed for so many years with Roshi at the helm, was collapsing, and no logic I perfunctorily grabbed was going to stop it.

In a dream I had two years after Katagiri died, I wandered the world homeless in one torn shirt and one pair of pants. At the end of the year I ended up at his vacant Japanese monastery in a cold gray cavernous, cathedral-like room. With hair matted, mouth frothing, eyes bulging, I stomped my feet and screamed "No" from my guts, and the whole building resounded. "I will not allow this. I will not accept the loss of this man." I woke up.

These shingles shocked and alerted me that I was not handling this new information well. As soon as the workshop was over, I cancelled everything and settled into winter on the lonesome mesa.

Each morning I went across to my studio. But instead of working or meditating, I sat in an old rocker, and the cinema just rolled. I played in my head the early mornings, the afternoons, the twilights I spent in the zendo in Minneapolis, Minnesota. The scenes came easily without any prodding.

Eleanor is sewing a black robe in the basement, humming to herself. Her chin has some chapped skin, and her fingers are nimble, quick. Another scene: I see them together in the hall. They flirt. Roshi says something. His smile could shatter an ice age. She laughs like sparkling champagne. I winced. It was obvious, right in front of us, if we'd paid attention.

I recall a talk he gave: a man is diving from a board one hundred feet high into twelve inches of water. Roshi had seen this demonstrated on a TV show. He loved to take popular media into a whole new dimension.

"No way from ordinary perspective can this man survive," he explains.

The diver had to transform into something flexible, holding no fixed idea that this feat was impossible. He had to become not who he was—or thought he was. His skeletal structure had to melt.

This sounds odd, funny, but Roshi was serious and enthusiastic, and I loved him for it. His way of seeing took me beyond my usual perceptions; boundaries liquefied; the world enlarged. I felt happy, whole. Naturally, his explanation might not have made logical sense, but neither did diving a long way into a foot of water. If you thought about it, it was a dumb thing to try to do.

That was the point. "My job is to make you very dumb," he often said.

"Dumb" in Zen was a compliment. It meant you weren't running ahead of yourself, planning, organizing, strategizing. You were open to receive the world as it was.

I could relate to that. A writer needed a certain dumb quality. I often told my students that in a downpour people rush for cover. A writer stands unprotected near a puddle, fascinated by the ripples the drops make, bewitched by the way they bounce on pavement, letting the rain hit her naked head. Both writers—and Zen students—needed to step into life fresh and experience it anew. Being smart was beside the point.

When I began studying with Roshi in 1978, there was not a lot of reading material on Zen. I guess we were more like Te-shan when he burned his books. We were sixties kids bent on direct experience.

Roshi didn't explain the practice; instead, we practiced it. It was hard physical labor to sit hour after hour on a cushion with our legs crossed. I experienced my conceptions and ideas melting into an intimacy with what was simply in front of me.

And Roshi was there, also sitting. Side by side, we practiced.

At the second lecture I ever heard him give, on a Saturday morning in June, he began, "I have been reading your Descartes."

I perked right up. Six years earlier I'd finished a master's degree in Great Books. At St. John's we were only to read the text. This impressed me. I was required to meet Socrates, Kant, Hegel, Spinoza directly, using no secondary sources. For a whole eight weeks in a two-hour seminar twice weekly, we wrestled with Descartes. What could this philosopher possibly mean?

Now so many years later, sitting up straight, what would this Zen teacher have to say on the subject?

"I think; therefore, I am," Roshi quoted Descartes's famous line. "I'm sure he knew, but forgot to mention," and here Roshi took a long pause, "I don't think; therefore, I'm not."

My mouth dropped open. In that moment all of Western civilization fell off a cliff. In that whole two-month class no one ever thought of that angle. We had tried every perspective to unlock Descartes's meaning. We leaned, exasperated, over that broad seminar table—there were eight of us and a St. John's tutor—and all we produced were thoughts on thoughts. That was a long July and a dry August in Santa Fe, New Mexico.

Roshi's simple statement, which seemed so obvious and ordinary to him, the slant to reality he'd lived with all his life, stripped my brain cells, flushed out my vision—at the back of thinking is nonthinking, on the other side of existence is nonexistence.

At the end of the lecture we chanted the *Heart Sutra* printed on cards. "No eyes, no ears, no nose, no tongue, no body . . . no color, no sound, no taste, no touch . . ."—we enumerated all these things and said they weren't. It was an antidote to the firm Western belief in our solid presence on the earth. No old age, no death, no stopping, no path, nothing to attain.

My time at that college, that study of René Descartes, prepared me to receive Katagiri Roshi's words when I heard him speak that late spring day in the green of Minnesota. This would have seemed crazy and very scary, but all that work at St. John's actually created a foundation. I understood the world would now be flipped on its ear, thrown over, belly-up. Nothing would ever be the same.

I stumbled out of that zendo with recognition alive in me, not from Descartes's thinking existence, but from Katagiri Roshi's nonthinking nonexistence.

I dove right into that deep pool of emptiness, moved across town to be within six blocks of Zen Center, and in a private meeting a few weeks later formally asked that man with a shaved head to be my teacher.

But eighteen years later on the mesa in Taos, New Mexico, staring out the window, I wondered what Katagiri Roshi really meant. Did he know what he was talking about? Maybe the diver on TV just had a trick up his sleeve?

IN LATE JANUARY PETER CALLED, and we compared notes. We were both dumbfounded. How could we have been that naïve? "I once drove home from a retreat at Hokyoji with Eleanor and asked playfully, 'Hey, how come I never hear about a boyfriend?'

"Right in the car she told me the whole truth. 'Oh, a while ago for over a year I had an affair with a married man, and it didn't work out. I guess I was disappointed and stopped after that.'"

We rehashed an early morning board meeting when one Zen student stomped in in his snow boots before the sun had even risen and demanded to know what was going on between Roshi and Clay. He had heard them at night in the house. This wasn't Eleanor. This was a student who came later, who adored everything Japanese, and she worshiped Roshi.

This went right over all our heads. There was a stunned silence. No one budged. Roshi looked straight ahead and finally whispered without even looking up at Clay, "You don't know what you're talking about."

Clay moved home to Lexington, Kentucky, and never came back.

I remembered how much I liked Clay. During the first retreat I ever sat at the Minnesota Zen Center in 1978, he sat next to me. I wanted to call him right then and say, "Clay, you're not crazy."

I cried a lot in that rocker. The shock finally shattered any veneer I attempted to create. I didn't want to know these things. I didn't want to know how human Roshi was; I didn't want to come up close and personal with him.

Sure, out of the corner of my eye I sometimes saw he wasn't happy. After the last retreat I sat with him, we drove the three hours back along the Mississippi to Minneapolis together. He'd been inspiring during the long hours of practice, and his daily talks had been vibrant, full of a generous vision of the world. He'd given his lectures after the evening meal, after a break, just as the last of twilight visited the farming valley where the monastery was. The rolling green hills, red barns, fields of corn and sunflowers, the Winnebago Creek slowly winding below the bluffs of the Mississippi, the insects lifting their voices—how idyllic could it get for this girl from Long Island?

The last night of that last retreat with him by the Mississippi I raised my hand and asked a question that bore little relation to what he'd been speaking about. The question had come up during the day—it was important to me—and it turned out it was the last one I ever was able to ask him in a formal teacher-student configuration (after a year's sabbatical he found out he had cancer). "Roshi, if we were living in Germany during World War II and we were Buddhists, how should we act?"

I felt the German woman sitting across the zendo from me tense up. She was in her mid-twenties. I hadn't spoken to her, since we were on silence all week. I doubt if I would have mentioned anything about this in an informal setting, but the long days of practice had cut to the heart.

Roshi spoke clearly into the kerosene-lit night: "Buddhism has no prescriptions. If your family is starving, and they hand you a gun and tell you to fight, you don't know what you'll do. That's why I tell you to practice. Maybe something fresh will come up."

The German woman began to cry. You could feel her relief. No standard condemnation. What space and freedom, a chance to let go and not be frozen in history. This was immense, compassionate, and simple.

But next to me in the passenger's seat driving home along the banks of the great river, Roshi seemed small, dejected, lost. He couldn't even respond to small talk, so I stopped trying.

Two Zen students were compiling his lectures for a first book with a publisher I knew. Roshi loved and respected books. When he was in San Francisco, he asked a student to drive him to a Japanese bookstore with floor-to-ceiling shelves. The student watched him walk down the aisles, stopping intermittently to run his hand along book spines, caressing the titles.

I knew he was afraid his talks weren't up to publishing standards, that no one would understand what he said. He thought his English wasn't good enough. This wasn't true. He made wild, wonderful, uncanny connections. I remembered one in which he discussed a tick in a tree patiently waiting for years for a warm body to pass underneath. And then plop! he demonstrated with his hands, it would drop itself onto the skin of a passerby.

My throat tightened. What had he been comparing this to?

Waves of anger rose in me. He encouraged me to open up. I was vulnerable. He held the position of teacher, but breached it.

At the time he gave that talk I made my own odd connections. I loved his lectures most of all. It was language turned on its elbow. Roshi was giving a true speech. I was becoming a true writer—

Was I willing to see true now? I'd rise to the challenge, speak in my studio to the space in front of me,

"Roshi, I'm deconstructing the way I idealized you"—
and then I'd stop.

If I let go of my solid vision of him, what would I
have? How dull the world seemed.

During our drive back to the Twin Cities, I broke the
silence in the car by suggesting to Roshi that I tell the edi-
tors of his book that it was not necessary to get formal
approval from him on finished chapters, that they should
just go ahead and trust their judgment. He sunk deeper
into the fake velour car seat. He was so relieved. He
couldn't bear to read his own words, though he told me
none of this. Instead, he just nodded in agreement.

When I helped him carry his sleeping bag and duffel
into Zen Center, he didn't look around or wave. I
watched his back as he walked upstairs to his apartment.

I had a glimmer then of the chasm between the Zen
master and the lonely, insecure man. That moment was
an opportunity to hold contradictory parts of him, to
understand life doesn't work in a neat package the way
I wanted it to. I could have come closer to his humanity—and mine. But I wasn't ready or willing. I had a
need for him only to be great, to hold my projections. In
freezing him on a pedestal I had only contributed to his
isolation.

I sat in the rocker, feeling sad and missing him.

He was the youngest of six children. His mother
barely had time for him. He'd spoken fondly of the single
hour that he once had with her when she took him

shopping. No other brothers and sisters. Just the heaven of his mother all to himself.

My mother was mostly absent in my life, not because she was busy, but because she was vacant. She woke in the morning, put on her girdle, straight wool skirt, and cashmere sweater, and then sat in a chair in her bedroom, staring out the window.

"Mom, I'm sick and want to stay home from school."

"That's fine."

The next day I wrote the absentee note for the teacher, and she signed without glancing at it. I was hungrier than I knew. I wanted someone to contact me, even if it was to simply say, "Natalie, you are not sick. That wouldn't be honest. As a matter of fact, you look lovely today." As a kid I needed a reflection of my existence, that I was, indeed, here on this earth. The attention I received from my father was invasive and uncomfortable. I hoped at least for my mother's affirmation, but there wasn't any.

Roshi was the one person who directly spoke to this hunger. When I went in for dokusan (an individual face-to-face interview with the teacher), we sat cross-legged on cushions, opposite each other. He wasn't distracted, "aggravated," or impatient. He was right there, which inspired me to meet him in that moment. I had friends, acquaintances I interacted with, and we sat facing each other across luncheon tables, but this was a man whose life's work was to arrive in the present. The effect was stunning. Life seemed to beam out of every cell in his body. His facial expressions were animated.

I could ask him a question, and he would respond from no stuck, formulated place. I think it was the constant awareness of emptiness: that although this cushion, this floor, this person in front of you, and you yourself are here, it isn't of permanent duration. Knowing this in his bones and muscles, not just as a philosophical idea, allowed him a spontaneity and honesty.

"Roshi, now that I am divorced, it is very lonely."

"Tell me. What do you do when you are alone in the house?"

I'd never thought of that. I became interested. "Well, I water the plants," I faltered, then continued, "I wash a few dishes, call a friend." The momentum built. "I sit on the couch for hours and stare at the bare branches out the window. I play over and over Paul Simon's new album about New Mexico—I miss it there."

His attention encouraged me. "Lately, I've been sitting at my dining-room table and painting little pictures." I looked at him. Suddenly my solitary life had a texture.

"Is there anything wrong with loneliness?" he asked in a low voice.

I shook my head. All at once I saw it was a natural condition of life, like sadness, grief, even joy. When I was sitting with him, it didn't feel ominous or unbearable.

"Anyone who wants to go to the source is lonely. There are many people at Zen Center. Those who are practicing deeply are only with themselves."

"Are you lonely?" I entreated.

"Yes," he nodded. "But I don't let it toss me away. It's just loneliness."

"Do you ever get over it?"

"I take an ice-cold shower every morning. I never get used to it. It shocks me each time, but I've learned to stand up in it." He pointed at me. "Can you stand up in loneliness?"

He continued, "Being alone is the terminal abode. You can't go any deeper in your practice if you run from it."

He spoke to me evenly, honestly. My hunger was satiated—the ignored little girl still inside me and the adult seeker—both were nourished.

I understood that Roshi too had been neglected in his childhood.

Even though he had tremendous perseverance, he was human, with needs and desires. All of us want something—even the vastly wise like a good cookie with their tea and delight in good-quality tea. Maybe it was that very perseverance that broke him. He couldn't keep it up, and his human needs leaked out. "Continue under all circumstances," he barked out, so often that that dictum even penetrated my lazy mind and became a strong tool for my life. But as I grew older I understood its drawbacks: if you are crossing a street and a semi is coming,

step aside. If you have hemorrhoids, don't push the sitting; take a hot bath. That one tactic—perseverance—can
put you on a dead-end road, and then what do you do?
Continue to march deep into a blind alley?

The hidden life of Roshi was being exposed. It took a
long time. The teacher who stepped forward was very
radiant. It was hard to see the darkness at his back, but
unless I could see his, I was vulnerable to being shortsighted in my own.

Touching Roshi's frailty finally brought him closer to
me, unraveled my solid grief. At the end of January I had
a painful backache that lasted all day. At midnight in my
flannel pajamas I got up out of bed, went to the window,
and looked out at the star-studded clear, cold night sky
with Taos Mountain in the distance.

"Where are you? Come back!" I demanded. "We
have things to settle."

I let out a scream that cracked the dark, but one raw
fact did not change: nothing made him return, and I was
left to make sense of his life—and mine.

I WAS BROUGHT UP in a culture that lived through World
War II. It was called the "just war," the righteous one, but
those who fought in it had seen things no one spoke of.
One friend's father was one of the soldiers who liberated
Bergen-Belsen. His wife said he didn't return the same
man. Besides his career as a lawyer, he was only interested
in the roses he tended each summer.

We had a country full of bewildered men who were bolstered by the fact that it was "a good war." But war was war, and they saw horrors, things that nothing prepared them for. How do you come back to red-lipped women in high heels and stylish feathered hats, to ice in tall glasses, tablecloths, bus stops, public libraries, neckties, and sidewalks lined with maples?

My father, an old man when we sat in the last row of a movie theater watching the invasion of Normandy, wept, reaching for tissues and clutching my hand. "I didn't know they suffered so bad over there." He had had it easy, dropping bombs from a distance on the Pacific theater. The truth was, for all my father's bravado I felt a powerful depression saturating him. My sister and I in our white and pink pinafore dresses turned somersaults, danced, and sang trying to get him to notice us, to cheer up, to be glad to be with us. We thought we were the cause of his unhappiness. No young girl could fathom the depth of those blues.

My generation was raised on something askew, not spoken of, and we felt it. Why did so many smart kids go so wholeheartedly and blindly into Eastern religions? We longed for something congruent, something that held up. How odd now to think I went to a man from the very country my father bombed. How naïve to think Roshi might not have had some of the same problems my father did from across the sea.

I've heard Roshi was depressed in the last years before he died. In some Zen circles in Japan there is an understanding that if teachers face a life-threatening illness in their mature years, their late fifties or sixties, and survive it, their depth is even greater than before. Roshi, my beloved teacher, did not pass through. I don't know if the "closed system," his attitude of silence, contributed to his early death. But how I wish in our desperation to keep him alive in the long, slow year that he was fighting for his life, one Zen student had bent close and whispered, "Speak. Unload your heart."

I am not saying repressed feelings are the cause of cancer. We live in human bodies that will die someday of one thing or another. Cancer is a disease. Some people die of it. Yet in the same way I urged my writing students, I could have urged him in hushed tones on his sickbed, "Whatever you need to say. Tell it all."

We tried everything else—chemotherapy, radiation, acupuncture, visualization—why didn't I, at least, grace him with what I shared across the country with so many thousands of writing students?

Perhaps I didn't ask him because I neglected to stop and ask myself the same question. "Natalie, what have you not come clean with?"

Maybe it's only now that I know the answer—or am willing to look at it. I left my husband. While his mother was dying of cancer and he visited her every day as she grew bone-thin, I went on Zen retreats. When his father died six months later, I signed up for a hundred-day practice period. Every morning I was gone at four o'clock to sit three hours before I went to work. Every evening I sat another two. On weekends I was at Zen Center sewing, pulling weeds, raking leaves, studying a passage in a dharma book.

My husband lost both his parents while they were still in their fifties. He had just turned thirty. Neither of us knew anything about death. I rang the bell in the zendo tolling impermanence while my husband wept, growing out of youth on our red couch in the living room.

He was the love of my life. When I met him, my heart fell open. Seven years after we met, three years after we took marriage vows, I divorced him. I walked out.

I continued to sit in the zendo in perfect posture, in the cool illusion of serenity, while a furnace roared at my back. Instead of feeling all the way down through my emotions in zazen, I split them off to escape my suffering. If fear came, I severed it. I fostered fantasy, daydreaming. I slept with unnamed men—one was a violinist, another a housepainter, a third an executive at Honeywell—and plowed under the intimacy I had known with Neil.

Fifteen years later I still missed him. Nothing changed, because there was pain in my core I wouldn't look at. Finally, I think I betrayed myself. Maybe that's what betrayal essentially is. We don't abandon someone else without forgetting part of ourself. I was split off from my heart center. I kept repeating my affairs out of desperation and took myself farther and farther from the source of my own love and well-being.

The worst was that Neil never knew how broken I was. He thought I didn't care.

Zen is about plunging oneself into the hot center of life and death. Nothing hidden, nothing not revealed. When there is a secret, the dharma can't grow direct from the root. It has to twist itself looking for sun.

Roshi's dharma heirs, the twelve priests designated to carry on his teachings, not only inherited his strengths, but also carried his shadow, the unclaimed, unseen part of their former leader.

Of course, we are drawn to teachers who unconsciously mirror our own psychology. None of us are clean. We all make mistakes. It's the repetition of those mistakes and the refusal to look at them that compound the suffering and assure their continuation.

Five years after the news leaked out, a former board member referred to Roshi as having "immaculate morality." I was surprised. I knew he knew better.

Having lunch with a dharma teacher, I was startled by her denial: "Oh, people exaggerate. It's not for sure."

Another Zen teacher at another lunch said, "In my day we didn't ever stand up to male authority. Good luck. What about his wife? You'll hurt her."

"I'm writing Roshi's wife to let her know what I'm doing. I don't want to hurt his family, but I also have to be faithful to the legacy he gave me: to write honestly."

Suddenly I could hear my mother's voice, "Why write anything? It only causes trouble."

A man on a Minnesota call-in public radio show asked me on the air: "I thought writers were supposed to tell the truth. I read your book after your teacher died. Recently I heard about some secrets, but you never mentioned them in your work."

"I didn't know about it then. I would have written it."

So I had to now, but I became increasingly nervous. I didn't want to injure anyone. This was the last thing I ever expected I'd have to face. I wanted him to live, even after his death, but in a real way. With Roshi I found Natalie. He gave me what I needed to stand up and go through this. This wasn't Roshi's story anymore. It was our story, the people who studied with him—and it's my story. It's part of how the dharma came to us. Nothing will ever change how this man opened my life. And not only mine—all the people who practiced with him were forever helped. We forsook him by freezing him in some pure image for our own selfish needs even when we had learned otherwise. To not be real about our teacher is not to be real about ourselves. It is to twist the dharma.

But I was afraid. I realized I would meet resistance. I began to doubt what I was doing. Was it right or wrong? The few lunches I'd had with Zen friends surprised me. Everyone was not going to applaud with "Good girl, Natalie." I had an abiding love for the people I practiced with. I didn't want to lose them.

Then something in me snapped. I had to face all this before when I confronted my father. This was familiar territory. No one was happy. My sister even laughed at me. Why was I making such a big deal? My family wanted to keep the idealized dream of who we were. Natalie, as a hurting individual, did not matter. All they knew was she was disrupting the plan.

I determined that anything I said had to be backed up. I had to know for sure as much as possible. I made a trip up to Minnesota. As I flew on the plane, I began to muse, to question things that had been hearsay: What was the actual story about Roshi's priest who lost his psychology license? What occurred and why? I was living in New Mexico when it happened.

I called the state psychology board when I arrived in town. They had to have the information.

"If he lost his license, it should be on the Web. Tell me his name. I'll look it up," said the receptionist.

Thirty seconds later, she was back. "Yup. He 'surrendered' it in 1990."

That was the very year Roshi died. I felt creepy. I wanted to hang up. This was none of my business.

"Surrendered? That's not the same as revoked?" I asked. Maybe he didn't care about being a psychologist anymore.

"Why don't you just come down and look at the file yourself. You'll have to give us a driver's license. Wanna make sure no one walks off with it."

"I don't need a psychology degree? I mean, I'm not a therapist."

"Nope, it's public knowledge. In fact, if you're coming today I'll just copy it for you so you don't have to wait. It'll cost four dollars."

I jotted down the address. Was I really going to do this?

I drove across the line from Minneapolis into St. Paul. The numbers suddenly switched, and I was lost. Didn't I have something better to do on a June afternoon? I felt like a snoop. I should have gone swimming in one of the city lakes instead.

I found the six-story board building and rose in the elevator to the third floor.

"Here it is," the receptionist reached out a six-page file before I even said my name.

I dug in my wallet and only had three ones and a ten.

She took the three. "Never mind. No one will know but you and me."

As soon as I left the building, I plopped down on the outside stairs and opened the file on my lap. It was half humid out. It was not yet the full flowering of a Minnesota summer. I liked this softer air after years in the dry Southwest. But at this moment I didn't care about the weather. I was not even sure I'd understand the jargon in the report.

I fumbled through the first page. He waived any formal hearing. I turned the page over. A client he had for two years had lodged a complaint. They'd gone out to dinner once and had a luncheon in a public place. A sideways hug, maybe a patted knee. Ordinary gestures, but this was a therapist and a client. Professional lines were blurred.

The licensee denied some of the accusations, said the hug was an encouraging display in a public place.

A breeze lifted the page I was reading.

None of us were very clear. I remember another therapist at Zen Center who gave me and Neil free individual therapy sessions. I knew she lingered after the hour visiting with Neil, so I pushed our conversation past the hour too. We were already separated. I heard she was getting a ride down to the next retreat in Neil's car. Something broke in me—I knew this was wrong, that it made me crazy, but at the time I knew nothing of boundaries. I called her screaming and crying. She did not console me. We never spoke again.

Many years later when visiting Minnesota I decided to confront her. Why carry around a rock in my heart?

She didn't remember the incident. She said, "I probably held the phone in my hand and wondered, 'Why is Natalie so upset?' It seemed back then we knew nothing of proper limits."

I was glad to have finally spoken to her.

A semi rumbled down University Avenue. I saw a meat hook painted in red and the letters "PRIME BEEF" in bright orange. Then the truck passed, and only a tangle of green trees across the street was left.

Were we all confused back then? I was a fledgling poet. Neil was a pianist. We held no professional positions, we could come in front of no board, but even before we took the vow of marriage, we said we could sleep around. What were we thinking? We knew that Neil's father had affairs, and we saw his mother's suffering. But we never translated it to our marriage.

Maybe we were all one big unhinged, bewildered fishy stew back then at Zen Center, but we thought Roshi was clear. He was not part of us, not part of our muddled humanity.

During our first retreat, Neil whispered to me, "This man knows who he is. He knows what he thinks. Who else can you say that about?"

On page six of the file: the licensee could be relicensed, but first he had to meet with an ethical consultant at least one hour per month for a period of two years. Five more pages of conditions followed.

My eyes fell on the word "religious." He had to "separate religious affiliations from the provision of psychological services."

I knew he never retrieved his professional standing. I think he wasn't interested. He went on to establish a Zen monastery.

I drove back to the Uptown area in Minneapolis near Lake Calhoun where I was staying, near where the center is. The whole two weeks of my visit I never went there to practice, but sometimes at night I walked in the alley behind the building. I saw weeds growing in the cracks of the sidewalk leading up to the entrance. It was now twelve years since Roshi lived there. I tried to recall what it was like, the heaven of it. Yes, with all the confusion, it was still the best thing I had ever known. I spent my thirties sitting still. At the age when others were investing their energy in building careers, a vast opportunity was presented to me— to meet my own mind and "to have kind consideration for all sentient beings every moment forever." That was a big job Zen and Roshi proposed, probably an impossible one, but it offered me an enormous vision of human life, so different from the one I was brought up with.

"Don't trust anyone. They're all out to get you," was often quoted by my father. I longed for a different perspective.

I could see the moon through the elm leaves. "Roshi, what I'm doing now is part of what you taught me. I want to see unfettered, all the way down. Who we were—what a human being is."

A mind that rests at zero. No good or bad. No criticism, blame—also no praise. That is how we were trained by Roshi. In a world of bonuses, competition, fear of failure, yearning for applause, receiving evaluations, grades, tests, reproaches, and condemnations, it was actually frightening to enter the zendo, where those things did not apply. Who was I, if I wasn't running after affirmation and dodging negation? A crow just crowed; a flower bloomed. Could I just show up at five each morning to sit for no reason?

"I'll be here whether you are or not. I'm not sitting for Minnesota Zen Center. I'm sitting for all sentient beings."

To wake up that early and to walk the six blocks to the center or to drive there, getting into my old car, parked on the street through the night in subzero temperatures—I could do it maybe once or twice to try to impress the teacher. But that motivation couldn't have sustained my effort. It was a waste of time anyway. Roshi wasn't impressed. And when I didn't show up, no one came to drag me out of bed or called to chastise me.

I'd wrestle with myself when the four-thirty alarm went off. "I'm going. I'm not going." Roshi called it "fighting with tofu." It's ridiculous; it gets you nowhere.

For the first three years that I practiced at Zen Center, I felt certain Roshi would kick me out. Finally, he would have to admit I was hopeless. I imagined my exit—it would be dramatic. I'd be sitting facing the wall, he'd run up behind me, scream, "I can't take it anymore," grab me by my collar and the seat of my pants, and fling me crashing through the window, wooden frame collapsing as I flew through.

Other times I envisioned him exclaiming to the whole group, "There is one enlightened one among you. Here, Natalie, please take my seat." And of course I would be gracious and humble, exclaiming to everyone there my sincere hope that they too someday—in some distant future—could realize the way.

It took those full three years for me to finally drop the need to be loved or maligned and to just appear. To accept that something in me wanted to be there in the same way a tree in spring sprouts leaves or a fish in water swims.

Often I told my writing students: "Look over your shoulder. No one's there. No one cares whether you write or not. You must step forward, pick up the pen, and begin." I'd smile. "If you do, maybe beings seen and unseen will help." Pause. "But don't wait around for that. Get to work."

I remembered Roshi said to me once in the dokusan room, "Look around you. The sangha [the spiritual community] is a microcosm of human society. You can watch it all right here."

Did he know how real that statement was?

I believe he did. Even betrayal was part of life. The whole sangha was going to die someday. Everyone I ever loved would sometime leave me. By not being willing to see things as they were I deluded myself. I was trying to hold out against reality.

THE NEXT DAY I LOCATED the phone number of the woman in Detroit whom Peter had originally told me about so long ago in that first phone call in California, the woman who had been Roshi's confidante. My heart raced as I heard the first ring. Don't be home, I thought. I can forget this. She's going to call me a busybody, a meddler. Let dead dogs lie.

On the third ring, a man's voice said hello. "No, this is her center, not her home. I can give her a message. Hey, aren't you the writer? Oh, she'll love to speak with you."

Oh, no, she won't, I thought as I hung up. So she has her own Zen place now.

The next day she called. She said we met once briefly five years ago.

I took a deep breath. "I want to ask you what happened with Roshi and the woman he was allegedly involved with."

"Oh," she paused. "I am happy to tell you.

"Yes, she was very unstable. They met in the Minneapolis Zen Center. She had slept with Tibetan lamas and other teachers before. She lost her job and moved to Detroit to live with her parents. At some point she was having a breakdown, and she called him a lot. He wouldn't answer the phone. Her frantic parents tried to call him too. This was when he asked me for help. He told me not to commit her. It might expose him. I was a therapist. He put me in an awful situation. Finally, I went along with his wishes, but then the woman called me all the time. She threatened to hurt my children. I was terrified."

She was talking faster than I could keep up. She was relieved to speak about it.

"People know you. They'll believe you when you write.

"After that I stopped practicing with Roshi. I'd had trouble with another Zen teacher. So I was crushed when this happened. I thought I could trust Roshi. I thought he was clean."

My heart sunk. Years ago I had heard she'd left the community. No one knew why, but the unspoken implication was that she wasn't a serious student. She had left silently to protect Roshi.

Hearing all this directly, rather than from intermediaries, gave it a clarity. I respected her forthrightness, and it urged me on. Suddenly, this investigation seemed so simple and direct. But I knew it wasn't. I was very alone. People wanted to minimize these events. We were all dedicated to our dream of him.

I remembered the effort it had taken to stand up to my father. I'd felt as if I'd taken on the whole institution of fatherdom. Everything had been set in concrete, and I wanted to budge it.

In the first letter I sent home, I told my father I only wanted to converse through the mail. I needed a way to protect myself. I was afraid I'd crumble if I spoke to him directly. As soon as he received the letter, he called.

"Dad, only through the mail."

"Natalie, that's ridiculous—"

I cut him off, "Only by mail. I'm hanging up." And I did just that. I'd shattered a universe. I was excited and amazed. You mean you don't have to do what your father wants?

While I was in Minnesota I also needed to find out if Clay's accusations about Roshi and his housemate at that early morning board meeting had any validity. Had anyone else ever seen or heard anything?

I could find no verification, so I decided to not mention the whole situation in my writing.

I was leaving the next day. The phone rang. It was an old Zen friend. We hadn't seen each other in years.

"Couldn't we at least go for a quick walk by the lake? I'll come around nine. You'll have time to finish packing."

I was tired, and the plane took off very early the next day. I hesitated, then gave in.

I was glad to see her, and the lake at night looked beautiful. She'd become a successful painter and showed at the Walker.

"So what are you writing now?"

I told her briefly.

"You included Maria, didn't you?"

"No, it's not for sure."

"Yes, it is."

I turned. City lights glinted off the water. "How?"

"I walked in on them. In the basement, where the washing machine was."

"You did?"

"Yeah, years ago when I first started practicing. The door had been shut and it was dark in there."

"What did you see?"

"I saw Roshi and Maria in an embrace. I had startled them and they looked like deer caught in the headlights."

"What did you think? Did you tell anyone?"

"I was embarrassed. I felt foolish. I didn't know what to think—I ran upstairs. I didn't mention it to anyone."

I slept little that night. The few blocks around the center had been home to me. They held so much.

When my husband and I were breaking up, Roshi told me to only speak to Neil when I could express myself clearly. I managed it on the phone every third day for short periods of time. I guessed it felt okay, but I had hurt, wrath, indignation underneath. I had loved this man, moved up to the strange Midwest to be with him, and it was all dissolving. In my early thirties, all passions warred in me. Now I was trying to be good on the phone. It lasted for three short conversations, and then the next time we spoke what I repressed exploded.

I described it to Roshi: it was as though a rabid red dog ran out of my mouth and bit my old husband's face.

"That's a good one." He laughed and laughed.

I was defeated once again and my emotions became a battleground.

With Zen practice I saw the difference between clinging rage and the red-hot wake-up of a flash of energy. I began to have an honest appreciation of anger's sheer reflexive, self-protective side and its destructive side; the anger that finally moves us, motivates us to change inwardly; the anger that is pure, like a first thought, comes through us, cleanses us, and passes. What was important for me was that it wasn't denied and shuffled off into a passive-aggressive mode.

But what I also understand now is that you can know about anger clearly with half of yourself while the other half is cut off and never gets the benefit of any of your clear knowledge. We've seen examples in great artists who are enlightened in their work and function cruelly and ignorantly in their personal lives. Unfortunately we have also discovered this about spiritual leaders. I think my generation hoped that Eastern teachers would be different, free of these problems, but the splitting off seems to be cross-cultural and across religions. No one is immune. Roshi was sincere about his vows, but in a split the one part doesn't live by the same rules as the other part. So a person could practice deeply, have great under-standing and aspiration for compassion, and simultane-ously act out in a way that blurs boundaries between teacher and student.

During a retreat I was finished with my dishwashing job, but the bell had already rung. Waiting until the next period in order to enter the zendo, I lingered in the kitchen popping spoonfuls of gomasio, toasted sesame salt we ground by hand, into my mouth.

Tony walked in, saw me, and screamed that I wasn't supposed to do that. Earlier that year after a lecture he had yelled at me for asking Roshi how he met his wife. He also said I wasn't supposed to do that.

I was startled by his aggression that afternoon. I felt vulnerable and tender after four days of silence and practice.

I didn't say anything. I went downstairs to the bathroom. When I came out, he was standing by the shoe rack.

"Tony, I don't know why you attacked me." I was hoping for some closure, for an apology so I could go back and sit in peace.

Instead, he attacked me again. "You do exactly what you want. You don't follow the rules."

Innocent me felt self-righteous. "Go to hell," I said and stormed up the stairs for the next sit. Wait until I tell Roshi. He'll comfort me. He'll protect me from that brute Tony.

Finally, my turn for dokusan arrived. I marched into Roshi's study, did my prerequisite bows, and then plopped myself on the cushion.

I told Roshi exactly what happened.

His response: stop causing trouble. He rang the bell for me to leave.

I couldn't believe it. I went back to the zendo and decided he misunderstood the situation. I waited for the last person to receive an interview, then I marched myself upstairs again.

I explained the whole situation again with more detail, the gomasio spoon, dishwashing, shoe rack. I enunciated clearly—maybe it was my English he hadn't understood. Maybe when I got upset my New York accent became heavier. (Of course, this had never been an impediment between us before.)

"You are a troublemaker. I know you very well. Cut it out."

"Roshi, you got it all wrong. It's Tony who's causing the disturbance."

"You and Tony are alike. Whenever you see commotion, you dive in."

I was never so insulted. Such injustice. I left the room, again marched down the stairs, and sulked.

It took ten years to see it a different way. I was telling my friend Eddie about it over lunch, explaining to him about the gomasio—I stopped. My brain flipped to a past page. Just that morning the cook had announced that all retreatants were to stay out of the kitchen, except for when they had jobs to do, and then he asked that we not eat any kitchen food except at meals. There had been a problem with pilfering late at night. I even had another vague memory: Didn't he say something about the gomasio supply dwindling?

I whispered across the table to Eddie, "I did start the whole thing. Roshi was right."

How could this man have been so clear, seeing into my

own nature, and then in another pocket of time been so unclear in his behavior toward some of his women students?

Several years after my divorce, Roshi assigned me the practice of not approaching those who hurt me with anger, but waiting until my intention was to create peace with them. I was older, calmer. I agreed. I'd already tasted the suffering from my breakup and didn't want to react blindly anymore. I knew those consequences.

Immediately after I made that promise, I encountered an old friend, the kind who manages to drop innuendoes about your weight, your lover, another friend, your writing. When you leave her, you're foaming at the mouth, gnashing your teeth, and you aren't sure why. After all, you were both smiling. You've known each other a long time. She was familiar, you have history together.

This time I went away from her as usual feeling like a maniac, but I had made a firm commitment to harmony. I didn't run back and start an argument. Instead, I held torturously steady inside myself. Peace, I hissed through my teeth, steam blowing off the top of my head. I felt as though I'd swallowed a whole crazed animal that jerked inside the container of my skin. She was trying to cut loose out of my arm—I saw the bulge try to break through my thigh, my chest, my belly. There it was trying to escape out my back.

Six weeks later—it took six hard weeks—I had a date with my old friend at a sushi restaurant for dinner.

Maybe I imagined it, but she seemed nervous. I think she honestly knew she'd blown it last time we'd seen each other. I felt spacious. We ate slabs of raw fish. I don't remember exactly what I said, but it was simple, short. I had no self-centered agenda, but I told her clearly I didn't like it when she said this or that about me and that I wanted to be able to honor our friendship. I do recall the awed look on her face, the respect, curiosity, surprise.

The miso soup was served. It was delicious, with small floating cubes of tofu and fresh chopped green onion. I was happy and at peace. I felt a great victory.

When I think back on my experience with Roshi at that one potluck at my house, it seems that he didn't think at all, that he never calculated any consequences. Another person stepped forward, the unknown, isolated hungry one. He even looked different—his skin was sallow as though he hadn't seen much of daylight. That person had been hiding away, perhaps waiting for a chance to have his needs met, however remote.

HE TOLD US WHEN he first came to San Francisco in the sixties he was appalled by all the unkempt hippies who sat with him. He said he would preach acceptance and then go up to his room and cry because he hated all these wild Americans. We seemed so strange.

That kind of real honesty was what I came to expect of him. It made his breach of trust even more shocking.

I've heard some men say, well, they were adult women—what's the problem?

We were not peers with him. It wasn't equal consent; it wasn't two independent individuals with a horizontal relationship.

Even if the women involved were okay with it, it was a betrayal of the community. Something hidden was going on.

Once I went to Roshi disturbed by Trungpa Rinpoche, a Tibetan meditation master I'd studied with in Boulder before I moved to Minneapolis. "Roshi, he was really terrific, but he had affairs with a lot of his students. I can't make sense of it. It felt weird." Trungpa's relationships were public knowledge, but they still crossed a primary boundary, and even in my naïve early thirties I was uncomfortable with it.

I cringe as I think of this interchange now. Roshi's reply: "Buddhism is Buddhism." I could tell by the straight horizontal line his lips made, his eyes looking ahead, that he was incensed by my question. He rang the bell with no further discussion.

I think it was the exact year he was having an affair with Eleanor. I was a sincere, albeit shortsighted, Zen student. What had I said that upset him? For a long time I contemplated the depth of that statement, "Buddhism is Buddhism."

One of the great things I felt around Roshi was that we were all equally seen and cared about. But was that true?

I questioned it now. Were some student connections more advantageous? Was he thinking about Eleanor when he was sitting? What went on during retreats when they had dokusan?

Eleanor was tall—almost six feet, highly freckled, fair, with shocking red hair and a noticeable mole above the left side of her lip—was that the type he liked? Did he find that darker brown spot on her face sexy? Why did he choose her and not continue to pursue me? She got more time with him. With all this in my head, my thoughts ran murky. I was glad I didn't know about it while it was happening. There would have been only confusion for me in the zendo.

But not knowing created misconceptions, a divide between what I thought was happening and what was really occurring. I went over endlessly in my head my connection with Roshi. I felt shattered, but I also began to feel the essential ground of my practice. I was glaring down inside the long narrow neck of what was:

Roshi, I'm calling you. Do you hear me? Get into form again. I want to speak with you, just one more time, and then I'll open my hand and let go.

I'm invoking you back into sight, sound, taste, back into color and smell, the felt world from whatever sawdust, ash, Huge Mind you have dissolved into, whatever task you are attending to in what other universe. Put down your dust rag, your job of cleaning the altar in another dimension, and be with me. We have to talk.

When you first died, I would have gone anywhere, climbed down into boiling water, crawled through vomit, swarms of biting insects to find you. But I would have been looking in the wrong places. Instead, I discovered you in your passion, need. In your human frailty I see you again. I might even have gone off searching for you in lofty places, heavenly realms, but all along the only spot I would really find you is back here on earth, in the raw meat of your swollen, agitated heart.

You taught me that it was in the continual meeting of yourself that we wake up, that we stay alive through clouds and sidewalks, trees and human eyes. Maybe it was the cancer, the being in America too long with no peers, having a secret so well hidden for so long that cut you off from yourself and separated you from everyone else. Added isolation to the original loneliness you were so good at talking about. My teacher of loneliness was lonely, alone with the Alone.

Oh, Roshi, what turmoil, but it spread farther than your own private heart. You passed suffering down beyond your death. One long black slash on your enormous life.

I feel you again in the thick snow of the Midwest, how it would fall all night and fill the streets, in the dark tangled branches before dawn along Irving where I'd walk to morning zazen, the streaks of early car wheels in the white street, the heavy gray weight of the sky. I walked through a mysterious world with some large assurance. I was in the heart of your teachings.

We came to you eager and open with our early confusion and a huge sincerity for finding the way. We must have been overwhelming. But I'm sorry, Roshi, you should have toed the line, let out an unequivocal scream in your bald head: NO! White-knuckled it if you had to, but left us alone. It's still unclear exactly what or who was involved, so no one knows the truth in its fullness.

I sense you were conflicted. Was this when you went to Japan and visited an important lineage teacher? Perhaps, you spoke to him about the American women—monasteries in Japan were all men. When you returned, you declared yourself celibate. I was living in New Mexico by then and thought it peculiar. I did not know then about your private life.

My generation longed for something pure, untouched, celestial. That was our mistake. Running from one disillusion, we jumped into the arms of another.

Roshi, how do I hold you now? More real, more honest. You gave me everything in those years when I lived six blocks away. My thirties, your fifties. The black terns on the September lake at breaks in autumn sesshin. When I sit or stand, I feel you. When I write, I hear you whisper, "Be yourself."

WE'VE HAD A LONG DROUGHT in New Mexico. Piñons have turned brown in the hills, their deep roots no longer able to find water. Great ancient cottonwoods that border the pueblo land and the road into town have given up. They stand now like ghosts of winter at the end of August. But this morning in middle September, it rained. I could hear thunder in the mountains and a pounding on the tin roof. The sage, the Russian olive at last showed their true turquoise color, and the chamisa bloomed its yellow pungent fall flowers. Snow was on the top of Wheeler Peak, the tallest mountain in our state. Its height has reached into another season.

Lung-t'an handed Te-shan the light, but then just as Te-shan was about to reach for the candle, Lung-t'an blew it out. And with that, everything was revealed. Night and day, fall and spring, the stars swirling in the open sky. What did Te-shan see in the new dark? His hand empty, he could not hold on to anything?

Did Roshi, knowing or not knowing, blow out our lights? Now we were on our own. Would we take advantage of this timely jolt from the other side, use it to wake up, or would we crawl under the warm covers in the dark and go to sleep?

LONG AFTER THAT SEASON that I ensconced myself on the mesa, I was at a conference in southern Arizona. I knew Eleanor lived nearby. I called her and made a date for dinner. What was it I wanted to ask? I'd always liked her, and I knew she was a serious practitioner.

We sat across a white linen tablecloth on a Thursday evening. We chattered about this and that. All the while in my head I urged, "Go ahead, broach the subject. You are a coward. Say something."

And then another voice sounded. "Shut up. What will you gain? Leave well enough alone."

One, two, three, I breathed and blurted out, "You know, I heard about you and Roshi."

The space between us froze. Her face became wooden—

At that very moment, the waiter appeared at our side. "Oh, goodness, you need rolls," and he shoved in front of us a basket of hot buns wrapped in a checkered cloth.

I reached for one. "Oh, they're good," I declared.

Eleanor quickly scooped butter into hers.

That bread had given me an escape. It was as though I'd never uttered a word.

After dinner I drove past tall saguaro cactus in my rented car to drop her off in front of her driveway. As I pulled away, I looked back through the rearview mirror. She had already gone inside. I knew she had loved him. I heard their laughter again filling the hall of the zendo. I wanted to feel a wild fury, but instead I felt heavyhearted.

A few months later the Minnesota Zen Center sent out a long letter referring to problems at Zen Center and the recently discovered indiscretions of the founding teacher. They were developing guidelines now to avoid these student-teacher problems in the future. But the language was so abstract, no one would have had any idea what it was about unless they already knew the situation.

Soon after it was mailed out, I ran into a longtime

Zen student in San Francisco. "I got a letter from Minnesota—I guess I'm still on their mailing list. I read it through three times, but I couldn't figure out what they were talking about."

I told him bluntly.

"You're kidding! I would never have guessed. From the letter, it never occurred to me that it was even about Katagiri."

Yes, none of us would have guessed. We were all in our own dreamworld of how we wanted things to be. Even when we knew differently, it was hard to face.

I think I finally freed myself in a single afternoon. I was already late, rushing to the plaza, with Taos Mountain at my back, to meet someone I didn't know. Glancing over at a big gallery window—usually it displayed large eccentric landscapes of a painter I loved—I saw that this time the window was empty. I halted in front of the glass. I put my hand to the pane. I don't know how to say this—in one stunning moment I fell through. I was in vast space. I wasn't myself. I was Katagiri Roshi, looking at Natalie. I experienced his love and admiration. I always thought it had been one-way, but he needed me as much as I needed him. I had believed in him. He couldn't have been a teacher without a student.

All of us in that small zendo across from Lake Calhoun had created something beautiful together. The love was equal; we all were part of the commitment and dedication.

Roshi wasn't some piece of heaven that marched through our midst and then left. Roshi, me, the students from Minnesota, the ones who migrated from Iowa and Tennessee, the ones who fell asleep on the cushion, the ones who came late, those who shaved their heads, who married, who showed up only to help at the summer rummage sale, even the floor, the walls, the breaking cold, the trembling early daffodils, the doorway, the altar—all were part of "dependent coorigination." He repeated the phrase often: nothing exists by itself. We were all interconnected and interpenetrated.

I wasn't less than Roshi; we were all good enough, ample, sufficient. Standing on this zero spot, this level, steady view, I could step forth and speak. Unfettered, I could let go.

PART 3

wife daughters friends this is for you
satori is mistake after mistake
—IKKYU

ON MARCH 1, EXACTLY NINE YEARS to the day that Roshi died, I drove up to Boulder, setting the cruise control at seventy-five, the Colorado highway speed limit. I was going up there to record *Long Quiet Highway*, the book I'd written seven years earlier about Roshi. This time there would be an addendum: what we heard about his relationships after he died.

I was adjusting the tape deck so the same song would play over and over. If I like a song, fifty repetitions are not too much. It drives passengers mad, so I reserve the pleasure for when I'm driving alone. I am of that lineage that lands one song and is happy to wire her nervous system to its beat, its words, the breath of the singer. I like those agonizing songs, the ones that shatter the mind and then link your life to something larger. In listening to a song like that continuously I'm carried to a bigger place. After that, no matter where I hear it—as background music in a café, in a passing automobile, hummed by a pedestrian on a busy street—my body splays open, and a huge world is available to me. Who else's songs can do this year after year but the Jew from the Iron Range in northern Minnesota, the alien in a cold place, who has seen some tough things?

This new car had a button I could press that slid the tape back over the same two feet of sound again and again. If only I could find it and coordinate the pressing of it with the end of the first play. Was that how it worked? Michèle explained it before I left.

I hunger for sound the way a wrestler wants touch. This is a five-hour trip. I need to fill my ears. I am focused on the buttons. I forget everything else.

I glance up. My car is heading for the side of the road. I jerk the wheel too fast to steer away from the shoulder. The car careens in circles, spins hard off pavement, hits dirt mounds, tangles in sage, eats up lumps of grass, then smacks against a big hill. My large green suitcase is flung out the back window with glass shattered everywhere, landing across the divider line in the south lane. In seconds, I am no longer in a car but inside an accordion. The backseat is caved in and the trunk is pushed up against me. In front an air bag is pressed on my chest. The tape deck is stuck on my one song: Bob Dylan wails, "Death is not the end" over and over.

I don't know if I'm alive or dead. I certainly am vacant of thought or feeling. I push open the door and crawl out. The hills are yellow and bare but for a bit of gray scrub. I sit on the side of the road. A van filled to the brim with a large Hispanic family pulls over, and they ask if I'm okay. I nod, and the mother with soft eyes sends her small son over to give me a can of juice. She knows I am not okay though my body is intact.

Some cars fly by. I just sit there. Finally the police arrive and tell me an ambulance from Pueblo is on its way.

Though I can walk, they strap me on a gurney, and as the ambulance whines down the highway, the technicians ask me questions. I know my date of birth, my address, even my Social Security number.

The driver calls back, "You don't look in your fifties. I thought mid-thirties."

I smile weakly.

I break down in front of two officers after being carried into the hospital. I tell them I am not appearing before a court in two weeks. "I can't drive up again. My car is all broken." They leave me alone with a forty-dollar ticket.

The X rays say I am fine. But I no longer trust my life, that it will stay with me.

Michèle drives up from Taos. We stay in a hotel that night. I only want Häagen-Dazs coffee ice cream and Coca-Cola.

So this is what a human being clings to when she's come a hair's breadth from death, I think as I spoon the dessert into my mouth. No great satori or sudden freedom? Just this. I feel the cold on my tongue.

The truth was I'd gotten two or three speeding tickets in the last six months. Outside of Española the police chased me for a full two minutes before I pulled over. I was blasting a tape so loud I hadn't heard the siren. Another time in Rinconada I tired of trailing behind three cars all dutifully doing the speed limit on a two-lane highway because a police vehicle was in front. I pulled into the left lane, jammed on my gas, passed the Goody Two-shoes vehicles at least twenty miles over the limit, and veered back into the right, ahead of the state patroller, gassing it even more, my taillights receding in his windshield.

Immediately, he put on his siren and flashed his red lights. I didn't care. I didn't want to be a good citizen anymore.

"Do you realize you almost hit a car coming in the other direction? Not to mention your speed." He leaned into my rolled-down window.

I glared at him. So what? I was a moment away from saying, "Fuck you." I imagined myself entering another layer of society—prison, detention, courts. Then shooting smack, sharing needles in back alleys. A grave restlessness reigned in me. It was as though I was between worlds—or pushing to enter some underworld. I'd left one, but hadn't been born in another. If there was no Roshi, what was there? The argument that Katagiri was the finger pointing to the moon didn't help. I didn't want the moon. But what did I want? I could watch my life slip away.

The day after my car accident, we stopped at the junkyard in Canyon City where they had towed my car. A thin man with gray hair and a Maine accent unlocked the gate.

"There it is," I pointed.

He looked at the heap of metal in the corner and then back at me. "You're not supposed to be alive," he whistled through his teeth, shaking his head. "Nobody gets out of a wreck like that."

On the trip home in Michèle's Jeep, every bump hurt. I kept repeating, "Slow down."

After Te-shan burned his books at Lung-t'an's monastery, he ventured on to wander through southern China. He heard that Kuei-shan's teachings were flourishing, so he traveled to meet him. But now Te-shan was an adept, someone who had seen into the heart of things, when that candle was blown out.

Carrying his bundle straight into the teaching hall, Te-shan crossed from east to west, back and forth. He looked around and said, "There's nothing, no one." Then he went out.

But when he got to the monastery gate, he said, "Still, I shouldn't be so rude." He wanted to bring out his innermost guts in dharma combat with Kuei-shan. He hoped to be challenged and deepened—tenderized.

So he reentered to meet Kuei-shan, who was sitting in the hall. Kuei-shan did not move. With full ceremony this time Te-shan greeted him, "Teacher!" Kuei-shan reached for his whisk, but Te-shan shouted, shook out his sleeves, and left.

Turning his back on the teaching hall, he put on his straw sandals and went on his way.

That evening Kuei-shan asked the head monk,
"Where is that newcomer?"
The head monk answered, "He turned his back on
the teaching hall, put on his straw sandals, and left."
Kuei-shan said, "Hereafter that lad will go to the
summit of a solitary peak, build a grass hut, and go on
scolding the Buddhas and reviling the patriarchs."

REMEMBER WHEN TE-SHAN met the old tea-cake woman when he had the pile of commentaries on the *Diamond Sutra* on his back? Now he carried a new bundle—the monk's—into the hall. He's still stuck, this time in the Absolute. He can't come down to the ground after the awakening he had with Lung-t'an.

At first he clung to his books; now he's attached to emptiness. Like a cat caught in flypaper, he roams the countryside looking for help. Kuei-shan could have helped him, but Te-shan couldn't stay still long enough.

Kuei-shan waited all the way till evening to ask after that strange monk. Unlike Te-shan, he was in no hurry. When the head monk said he left, Kuei-shan made a pronouncement, but saying that he was going to go to an isolated summit and rail against the lineage was not a compliment about Te-shan's future. Kuei-shan was saying that Te-shan, no matter what insight he recently had, was still upholding the pattern of his suffering. He continued to be distant, fervent, caustic. It doesn't mean that having understanding causes one to suddenly become someone else, all at once a tender sweetheart. A person has a bundle of qualities that make up his or her character, but these sets of energies, if that person is lucky and is filled with inspiration and effort, evolve. Sometimes for better—or worse.

Te-shan's whole lifetime way of meeting the world was understood by this old teacher. Te-shan here was still living in a cave and not free. In this quick meeting, he was seen through by Kuei-shan.

I COULD NO LONGER quite trust any teacher I studied with, not in the way I had been devoted to Roshi—and I still hadn't lodged that trust deep in myself. I could not settle down.

In April, a month after the car accident, I traveled to Florida. I was to be a speaker at a book fair in Palm Beach. This was near my parents' home, so they came along, but of course I didn't tell them about the car accident, in the same way I didn't tell them about the mugging in St. Paul. It would have upset them.

Behind heavy curtains on the stage of the convention center my father discovered tables of brownies, punch, small sandwiches, Danish. "Nat, it's free." He held up a can of Pepsi. He'd already eaten three rugalach. "Free," he repeated. "Free."

"Yes, for the volunteers and presenters," a woman nearby in diamond-studded glasses and a T-shirt with a glittering palm tree chimed in.

"Yes, and for their parents," my father twirled over to the cheese display, undeterred even for a moment.

He was so happy that he almost bought a book later when we walked around on the main floor peering into stalls.

"Young man," he said to the owner of a small press, his hand clamped on the Midwesterner's shoulder, "I'd like to purchase something, but my daughter here is a published writer, and I still have her books to read."

Then I could hear his loud whisper, "Free food behind that wall," and he pointed with his thick finger.

My mother was about to buy a bookmark farther down the aisle. He scurried up. "Syl, we don't need that. Here," he withdrew a cocktail napkin from his pocket. "Just use this to hold your place." He smiled broadly. "Look, it's got the name of this fair."

My mother, flustered, let go of her purchase.

For almost the whole visit my father was in high spirits. One night in their living room, he put on a show of different characters. Disappearing into the hall, he returned with a black patent leather matador hat on his head, and he waved a dishrag in front of himself, repeating, "Bolero." He was enticing a bull into the dining room. For act two he hobbled over to us like a bum, wearing an old brown felt fedora and a plaid wool jacket. For his final act, he was Sherlock Holmes, pipe in his mouth, checkered hat with flaps tied at the top, visor in the back and front. He held a spyglass to his eye, inspecting the couch for clues to crack the crime. Then he came over to my hair.

"Let's see what this dandruff reveals."

"Daddy," I yelled, trying to grab his hand, and fell into peals of laughter.

The last night of my visit we went to the Gourmet Deli, the scene of my famous second dharma defeat years before. It was a mile from their house. We had had such a good visit I almost forgot the recent car accident and the pain and fear I still felt. We'd already ordered when my father leaned in close.

The weight of our imminent departure (Michèle had come with me) was on all our minds. "I'm going to miss you" is what I expected him to whisper. I bent to hear what he had to say.

"You need to lose weight," he hissed in my ear.

I shot up in my seat, tears sprung in my eyes. Was that what he was noticing all week? My father, always overweight but not caring, carrying it with a flair, had dropped decades of pounds since his operation almost a year ago.

I was speechless, hurt to the core. I couldn't look up. I picked at my hamburger. Our last meal was a tragedy. The bill came, and I ran to the car.

My father wasn't quite sure what he'd done. I told him he should apologize, my weight wasn't his business.

When we came home, he just stared at the TV.

The next morning I phoned them from the airport.

"Are we still pals?" he asked. I knew this was as much as I would get.

"Yes," I hesitated, "but I'm not fat."

In late July every time I phoned, my sister, who was visiting, and my mother were always out shopping. Usually my father never picked up the phone. If no one else was there, he'd let it ring. (They never owned an answering machine.) I think now he felt the weight of his loneliness.

"Oh, Nat, when are you coming?"

"Remember—this Monday, August 2."

"When's that?" My father in the last two months had become confused. "Gee, I hope I last that long."

"You will, Daddy." He'd never said anything like that before.

For the last weeks he'd been sleeping a lot—and in the bed, not dozing in his blue TV chair.

Sunday morning he woke up to go swimming as he always did. Then he decided not to go.

Sunday afternoon he'd told my mother to call 911. He didn't feel well. When the paramedics came, they took his vital signs. They were all fine.

"Take me anyway," he said. "I'm not well." This was not like my father. He hated hospitals.

In the ambulance he had a heart attack. Not a bad one, they said.

As soon as I arrived Monday night, I drove to the hospital. He was sedated, tossing his head back and forth, his hands tied down. They had tubes in his nose. Even unconscious, he was trying to pull them out.

I sat beside him a long time. Then I noticed he wasn't wearing his ruby ring.

The next day my sister kept repeating, "I don't understand. It's the doctors. They did it to him."

A few days before, they'd gone to the beach. She told me that out of the blue he turned to her while driving and said, "You know, Romi, everyone has to die someday."

"Not you, Daddy." She clutched his hand.

"I'm sorry. No one gets away," he shook his head.

All kinds of monitors buzzed and clicked.

"What can you do?" my sister grabbed the nurse's arm. "His kidneys, I saw the monitor screen, they're getting better?"

The doctor came in. We all stood around my father's bed.

"Well," the young physician in white sighed deeply. He'd seen this before. "His kidneys aren't functioning—"

"They will, though, they will." My sister held a fistful of the white sheets.

My mother backed away from the bed. She was afraid of hospitals, of my father like this.

His legs hung out of a thin pale hospital gown deco-
rated with small blue diamond shapes. His feet were
beautiful. All the swelling from bursitis was gone. But
this was not my father tied down like this. He was full of
small motions. Sometimes his eyes fluttered open, but he
wasn't seeing.

Have I said his eyes were blue? Yes, they were blue,
but now they were vacant.

Michèle and I went back to the hotel in late afternoon. We dropped my mother off at home. My sister
stayed, trying to convince the staff to get his liver up and
going. "Just two days ago we swam in the waves," I
heard her say. "It's this hospital that did it to him. Now,
please, fix it."

I sat on the beach in early evening. This was it.

Early the next morning the phone rang. "Daddy is on
life support."

"I'll be right there."

Now he was breathing into an aspirator.

"Romi, we have to let go. There's nothing we can do."

"Let's meet with doctors. Hear what they have to say."

She didn't get it, but I didn't roll my eyes. That would
mean I still possessed irony, humor, sarcasm. Instead, I
was as dull as lead, but in a sudden moment of inspiration, I actually addressed my father directly. The only
time anyone thought to do this. I bent low and spoke into
his ear, "Daddy, is there anything we can do?"

From the depths of another world, he breathed out one singular last human word, "No-o-o-thing."

I thought I might be imagining it, but the nurse tucking in his sheet repeated it. "See, even he knows."

We meet in another room again with the young doctor.

Without saying he's as good as dead, he tells us all his organs have given out. He suggests hospice. He makes a call on a beige phone.

"So how long will he be there? Three months?" my sister asks.

I'm watching all this now as if it were a play. I know as soon as the plugs are pulled, he will be gone.

"Romi, we have to let him go," I tell her.

The doctor turns to my mother, "Mrs. Goldberg?"

"Well, whatever you say."

"It's over." I look straight at my mother. She doesn't look back.

"How do we proceed?" I ask the social worker, who has joined us. It is clear we are taking him off life support.

My sister pleads, "Well, maybe we don't know he could go the other way."

"Each of you individually can go in and say good-bye, tell him what you want." I watch her thin neck working up and down as she speaks. She's wearing a gold heart on a narrow chain.

My sister goes down the hall first. She comes back sobbing, her small nose bright red and pale around the nostrils.

I go next, tears running down my cheeks. His large head cocked to his left shoulder, he's on his back, facing the ceiling. I observe the stubble over his paunchy cheek, the pale eyelashes, his receding hairline, and steel gray hair. He is still handsome. He can't be a man subject to the laws of life and death. He must be something else, an avalanche. But here it is: my father is dying, his last tumble in all his years. My words blow breath on his long earlobe. "Daddy, I've come to say good-bye. You can let go and go on. I have always loved you. Take my love with you. I love you." I repeated those three words over and over. "Thank you for being my father. I'll miss everything about you. You were a great man. Thank you for my life. Everything is complete. Go on." There was a slow tear rolling down his right cheek. "Forever I'll love you."

I leave and walk down the empty hall. Michèle passes me on her way in. She's known my father for two years and wants to pay her respects.

Then my mother goes in and comes out. The male nurse beckons us back. We stand around the bed. We all touch him—I hold his right foot and leg—as the nurse undoes the wiring and tubes.

"It's so final," my mother whispers. I put my hand on her shoulder.

When the wrist restraints are untied, the full life of my father roars out and fills the room. He is a wild thing, a white lion. He arches his back and faces the window, the death rattle comes from his throat, and he is free, gone. He does not look back; he does not linger. You feel it. Something much brighter than this life calls him, and he charges on.

I know death will never scare me again. It isn't some foreign dark cave at the end of life. It is the most natural, ordinary thing. It is as though a hand turns over from palm up to palm down, or a leaf flutters and we glimpse its silver underside. It is almost as if nothing happens— the big emptiness is just there as it always has been.

Ben Goldberg was merely a squiggle on open space— his love of Bing cherries, horse racing, the odd funny twist of his humor, the year of his birth, 1916, the first woman he loved, the last time he ate rye bread, saw Brooklyn, drove a car—all dissolved. We, human beings, his daughters who stood by his deathbed, wanted to believe he was forever, solid and dependable. Not so. He had passed on. My father, whoever he was, was gone.

It was four in the afternoon. A blue sky and palm trees lined the boulevard outside my father's window. When the service sent him to Miami to teach swimming to the officers, he never got over the place. After the war he returned to New York and told his mother about the flamingoes, the white buildings, the forever summer. He brought my mother down here on their honeymoon. Now he ended up in his paradise. He'd made it.

Michèle drove my mother home. My sister and I sat for a short while in the room. I knew about being with the body to help the soul on its journey, but clearly the man had moved on. No spirit was hovering in this hospital.

BACK AT THE HOTEL late that night old, past fears ignited. I'd learned to control my father by putting up fierce boundaries. Now he had no body. He was amorphous. He could creep into my bedroom, and I did not know how to block him.

Suddenly it felt as though his death left behind vapors. That creepy part of him descended like smoke, surrounding me with a putrid smell.

The week before, I'd sent a present to my sister at my parents' home. My father blithely told me on the phone he'd opened it.

I clenched the phone's mouthpiece. "You have no right." Nothing had changed.

He laughed. "It's no big deal. I just wrapped it back up."

I was helpless all over again.

THE NEXT DAY we went to the funeral home. His body would be refrigerated and flown up to New York the following Monday. We'd have a graveside ceremony at the old Hebrew cemetery in Elmont, Long Island, where the family owned a plot. Even his parents had been buried there in another area a long time ago.

My sister, mother, Michèle, and I would first go that

Sunday to a cousin's wedding in Westchester, New York, and the following day all the relatives, conveniently gathered, would drive out for the funeral. Much discussion ensued about exactly where in the plot Buddy's body would be placed. Not next to Aunt Priscilla, but it would serve her right. She once put him down when he used a big word, "You don't know the meaning of that," and he never forgot it. Now the snob and the man who never finished high school could duke it out in heaven. But if not there, he'd have to lie next to Grandma, my mother's mother, and he wasn't a blood relative. Besides, wasn't Uncle Manny, her favorite, going to be laid there? And then Cousin Nancy wasn't even sure in thirty years that she wanted to be buried in New York. So another potential space opened up.

We chose a plain pine box, not because my father was Orthodox, but because it was cheap. My father had said, "Don't spend money on my coffin. Just another way they can rip you off." It was exactly like the one that they had cremated Roshi in nine years earlier. These simple boxes are often used by Orthodox Jews for burial. The Zen students removed the Star of David from Roshi's and saved it for me. This Jewish star attached to my father's coffin would be buried with him.

IT WAS A BEAUTIFUL Monday in August. Not humid, not hot, but the sun shone, and we could hear the shouting at

Belmont Park, a mile to the north. It was the fifth race of the afternoon, and the Thoroughbreds were making their last turn into the homestretch, when the limousine pulled up with my father's body. I'm sure he strained through the black metal of the long car to hear who'd won. But more likely he was hovering over the track right then, angelic arms outspread, mouthing in a whisper like a green breeze, "Four-legged animals, turf, jockeys, silk shirts, bets, hopes, dollars, tickets, bleachers, outdoor stands, men with cigars plugged in the corner of your mouths, and women with brassieres, nylons, and high heels, adieu, adieu."

Meanwhile, his family stood empty-handed around the box they were lifting out of the back hatch. The man in charge needed a witness, someone to look in one last time and make sure they shipped the right corpse to the right place.

My sister and I stepped forward. His face looked like wax. His beard hadn't grown. Looking straight up, his eyes were opened, the blue incandescent.

My sister talked nervously to the attendant. "He looks like a sculpture. I was an art major in college twenty years ago . . ." and she started to tell him about using clay for modeling.

He had on the blue silk Hawaiian shirt that he refused to take off for a full month after I bought it for him. We'd given it to the undertaker. Now he could wear it forever.

"It's him," I nodded, and they closed the lid.

Relatives piled in cars to drive the length of three city blocks to the grave site. I walked there slowly, the way I'd been taught by Roshi. Mindful of each step, I repeated, "This is your father you're burying today. This is it."

But it felt more as if I was in someone else's movie. Whose father? Whose daughter? What town? You know someday your parents will die, but it's always a future occurrence. I passed gravestone after gravestone, old upright aging markers with Hebrew characters carved with filigree and hearts.

Everyone was gathering in front of plot eight. The hole was already dug and the dirt piled high. My mother and cousin Esther sat in white plastic chairs Michèle and I had purchased at a neighborhood grocer before the ceremony. A local Reform rabbi was there to perform the service. I told him that I would take over. Then I asked if anyone had anything to share about my father.

One cousin recalled the way he loved to buy fresh roasted chichi nuts from a vendor in New York.

Esther told how he took her husband, Venty, to a strip joint the night before their wedding. That he dragged him to a front-row seat and gave him two singles to put in the stripper's cleavage. She turned to me. "Your father loved to shock people."

A great-niece recalled how he pulled her out of bed one very early morning when she was visiting to take her to the pier in Lake Worth to watch the seagulls and the fishermen, how when they passed young boys eyeing her, my father put his arm around her shoulder and told them, "She's my wife."

My sister read a poem torn from a notebook. It was about how she would miss her father.

My mother said he was a wonderful son-in-law to her parents.

I read from a book I'd written about painting, what it was like to sit in front of my father and draw him.

Then the coffin was lowered into the ground. The leaves on the old sycamores lining the walk tilted in a slight current of air. I knew it was no longer Benjamin Goldberg, but it was also that man, the last of him in this life.

The rabbi now wanted to say Kaddish. He had mentioned earlier to me that it is traditional to throw dirt in after the coffin, but it was too emotional, so he wasn't going to ask anyone to do it. I held up my hand for him not to begin just yet. I stepped forward, bent down, grabbed loose soil in both my hands, lifted the soil to my mouth, kissed it, then released it over the opening in the earth. My sister was right behind me. Wasn't this how it always was? The younger sibling following the older. The rest of the family took turns with the small shovel. Some held back. The two widows in their eighties continued to sit in their plastic chairs.

I nodded to the rabbi. He recited the ancient Hebrew. People cried. I held another position—the guide at my father's farewell. I did not cry again for months.

It was over. We all lingered. The sweetness of being together. Life was hard—and now there was one less. We handed out Pepperidge Farm cookies I picked up when we bought the plastic chairs.

I heard the gruff sound of someone clearing his throat. I looked up. Three men in plaid shirts, leaning on shovels, dirt on their faces, were waiting at the edge of the plot.

"Oh," the rabbi tried to shoo us away, "they're on union time."

"Go ahead," I nodded, and they stepped onto our grave property and dirt flew. In moments the hole was filled.

Most of us drove on the Long Island Expressway headed for the heart of the city, straight to the Carnegie Delicatessen. A long table in the back was reserved. We ordered thick pastrami and corned beef, tongue and brisket piled high on rye, specials—those big hot dogs my father loved—coleslaw, kosher pickles, potato pancakes, one plate of cheese blintzes. My sister wanted chicken soup with matzo balls. We had a plate of herring in sour cream, many RC root beers. With each bite someone pledged to my father.

"Buddy would have loved this."

These were second cousins, nieces, nephews, a first niece-in-law, his two daughters, his wife. No aunts or uncles, no brothers or sisters. They had long passed away. At the table sat the generation of American Jews who'd gone to college, donned running shoes, and lived in Westport, Manhattan, Boston, or Westchester. Uncle Buddy, even if he wasn't truly their uncle, was the one who introduced them to this food from the old country of Brooklyn. It was their touch with the past. He didn't know what a fax, a cell phone, or a computer was all about—and he didn't care.

We chomped on rugalach and bobka for dessert.

"Wait a minute! Wouldn't he have liked some strawberry cheesecake?" We ordered half a cake.

Across the table Michèle looked green and excused herself. I followed her to the bathroom.

"I've been nauseous all evening, ever since I drove you, your mother, and sister from the cemetery."

Walking back to the table, I knew sometimes it took the outsider, the non–blood relation, to witness and carry the suffering that is in the back of every relative's mind.

My mother, after a lifetime of good health, fell apart. She had spinal stenosis, then bad teeth, then heart palpitations. Cataracts were removed. She had glaucoma. Whenever she was lonely, she called 911 with a new ailment. None were fatal; some couldn't be corroborated upon examination and testing. Still, she was in pain, and she'd never been alone in her life.

A person went to work and came home. He went on vacation and returned. He went to the bank and drove the same streets, again to reappear. He went to his death—maybe the wait was a little longer, but the coming back was programmed into me. I wasn't fully grieving. I was on standby. But two springs had flowered, almost two summers had passed in which he did not swim, two birthdays when he did not age.

Hiking in Bandelier National Park outside of Santa Fe one Saturday when dusk came and the visitors had to leave, I did not want to go with them. The presence of an ancient people among the pueblo ruins was palpable. Finally, a forest-service ranger politely addressed me directly, "The gates will be closing soon down by the entrance."

I thought of hiding behind a boulder where a yucca was growing, then reluctantly obeyed the law. But I could not drive the hour and a half home. Something compelled me to linger. I stayed in a cheap hotel in nearby White Rock and slept long into the next morning.

I hadn't planned to be gone overnight. I had no toothbrush. I splashed water on my face, slipped on the same clothes I wore the day before, and headed back to Bandelier.

During the night I had dreamed that my father slept next to me, and I told him to rest, that I would take care of things now. It was a simple dream, but it was the first I'd had of him in the long months since he died.

Instead of hiking down through the falls, I turned right toward Frijoles Canyon. Thirteen years earlier was the last time I backpacked down there with my friend Frances. We camped near red cliffs and a cold stream. We'd seen deer, and I wrote the pivotal chapter of a book in which I clearly enunciated what wild mind was. All at once I had to find the ponderosa I leaned against when I wrote. I hadn't eaten breakfast. I had little water, no food. Could so much have changed in all these dozen years? Where was the meadow where Frances told me she realized she loved David, the man she eventually married and divorced? Where was the high narrow cliff we circumambulated, the knife we lost in the tall weeds? I pushed on at a furious pace way beyond where visitors were treading that day. Perspiration poured down my face. My feet hurt, and my socks were stiff with sweat.

Breathing heavily at the top of a thin incline, I stopped. What was I really looking for?

Wild mind, I had written, was outside our normal perception, beyond our constant discursive thoughts, as big as the sky. All we need to do is take one step backward, and we live in that mind, one with everything, not limited to the boundaries of our skin. It is the place where birds, clouds, old memories, horses move through us.

My heart fell into my stomach. I was out there looking

for my father. I wouldn't find him in the old way. He'd gone beyond being a human being.

Exhausted, I turned back toward the trailhead.

All the rest of that summer I hiked up to Heart Lake north of Questa, up Elliot Barker Trail toward Angel Fire, Divisidero off Cañon. I spotted a herd of thirty to forty elk through my binoculars off Latir Mesa way up above Cabresto Lake. I sat and watched them for a full hour.

That spring I had dreamed that elk came to me, and the biggest one, the leader, tried to break into my house. I was afraid and hid under a table with my friend Wendy, who also in real life had lost her father. Finally, I let the big elk in, and we sat opposite each other. He tried painfully to communicate, but we didn't speak even close to the same language.

When I saw the herd that afternoon in late summer, I felt peaceful and at ease. I knew I had found my father again.

One day Te-shan descended to the dining hall, bowls in hand. Hsüeh-feng asked him, "Where are you going with your bowls in hand, Old Teacher? The bell has not rung, and the drum has not sounded." Te-shan turned and went back to his room.

Hsüeh-feng brought up this matter with Yen-t'ou. Yen-t'ou said, "Te-shan, great as he is, does not yet know the last word."

> *Hearing about this, Te-shan sent for Yen-t'ou and*
> *asked, "Don't you approve of this old monk?" Yen-t'ou*
> *whispered his meaning. Te-shan said nothing further.*
> *Next day, when Te-shan took the high seat before*
> *his assembly, his presentation was different from*
> *usual. Yen-t'ou came to the front of the hall, rubbing*
> *his hands and laughing loudly, saying, "How delight-*
> *ful! Our Old Boss has got hold of the last word. From*
> *now on, no one under heaven can outdo him!"*

THE LAST TIME we see Te-shan in the ancient texts he is an old man and an able teacher. He has his own monastery with many students and is renowned for his non-verbal teaching. This philosopher of the *Diamond Sutra* became a master who taught almost without words.

When his students came to him, he energetically used the kyosaku, the hitting stick, which Americans are horrified by and associate with the toughness of Zen. Te-shan would say to his students, "If you speak, you get thirty blows. If you do not speak, you get thirty blows."

But Te-shan was not a maniac who arbitrarily cornered his students and beat them. By now Te-shan was a seasoned teacher, not stuck in the wandering heart of the young man who journeyed to see Kuei-shan and then left immediately. His character had matured during the thirty years he lived in obscurity after the visit to Kuei-shan. During this time his taciturn, stern nature allowed him to develop a presence of penetrating silence. Now he had become the teacher of Hsüeh-feng and Yen-t'ou, and out of his lineage would eventually emerge the Yunmen and Fayen schools.

These blows were more an expression of the Middle Way—words, but not words. What is the sense of what he is saying? He'll hit you either way, speaking or not? You're thrown back on yourself.

In our final meeting with Te-shan, he is heading toward the monastery dining room, his eating bowls in hand.

Hsüeh-feng, who is the cook, sees Te-shan from the kitchen. Hsüeh-feng is an ardent student who has not yet attained realization. He calls out, "Where are you going with your bowls in hand, Old Teacher? The bell has not yet rung."

Te-shan simply turns and goes back to his room.

No fight. No reprimand—how dare you talk to me like that? No correction—why is the meal late? Understand: Te-shan did not suddenly become a doddering pushover. He was capable of immense power, but he did not need to exercise it anymore. He was deeply at home in himself, in harmony with the universe.

There is a saying in Zen: a pearl rolling in a silver bowl. A smooth ride, no bumps, no jagged edges. No resistance, no fight, desire, need. The precious metal and the gem meet perfectly.

This rolling pearl was the mind of Te-shan at the end of his life. It contained multitudes—contradictions, paradoxes, life, and death all were embraced. Nothing caught him or tossed him away—or perhaps he was completely tossed away, at one with all things.

The story goes on a bit with an effort by a fellow monk, Yen-t'ou, to help enlighten Hsüeh-feng, the cook, who misunderstood Te-shan's simple turning as an example that the old teacher was failing. But it's not necessary for us to go on. We can end with our friend, turning in the hallway, his bowls in hand, open, surrendered, at ease, living in vast acceptance. We all know the one hard road he traveled to find himself here.

IN MAY, ALMOST THREE YEARS after my father's death, I visit my mother, living alone in Florida, now eighty-six years old. She is very thin, walks slowly with a cane, and has trouble seeing.

I'm telling her some grievances I had from the past. (I seem to never give up.) I'm sharing in the hope of closing the distance between us. I'm trying to see my father's absence as an opportunity. Death will also claim her, and I want some reconciliation before she goes.

She is hard of hearing. I have to speak loudly even though I am sitting on the couch across from her. The discussion is not going well. She bristles and denies anything but the glorious childhood she perceives that I had.

She affirms her position with an example. "Don't you remember when you were inducted into the Junior Honor Society? I was so proud."

I am not deterred. I push ahead. I know this is my last chance. "Mom, my memory of that day is that you were arguing bitterly with Daddy and your only comment to me was, 'You are the only pleasure I get.' You didn't really acknowledge *me*."

I know I am going over her head. A daughter of immigrants, my mother has three basic concerns: Did you eat? Did you sleep? Were you warm? Psychology is a field that developed in another country, not Brooklyn.

She is quiet. We are at an impasse. I do know that in the last years by herself she has mulled over her past, grieved her mother's death that happened almost twenty years ago.

"Why didn't I fly up when the nursing home called and said Grandma was fading? What was the matter with me?" She has cried herself to sleep many nights in the lonesome bedroom.

Now she turns to me. "Natli, I was a very unhappy woman. I think your father was having an affair."

My eyes widen, my head jerks. I was not expecting this. I sit up straight. Did I hear right? "What?" I ask, incredulous.

She nods. "With Ruth. Remember the barmaid who worked at the Aero for twenty years. She still sends Christmas cards. When your father's hands were too shaky to write her back, he'd ask me to. He was always worried about her arthritis. Oh, he was so happy when he heard she was feeling better." My mother makes a face.

"Wait a minute. What makes you think—"

"I'm sitting here realizing what a dolt I was. Your father always worked Tuesday nights—do you recall? They closed the bar at four, but sometimes he didn't get home till six thirty.

"I'd say, 'Buddy, where were you?' He'd say, 'I had some drinks with the boys.'

"After she was working there a year, we came home from visiting you up in camp, and there was an unsigned letter in the mail for me. 'Where is your husband on Tuesday nights?' was written with a pencil in a terrible handwriting. I showed it to him, and he said, 'It's one of the guys pulling a prank. Give it to me. I'll figure out who it was and get even.' He acted indignant. I handed it over and never thought about it again. But, let me tell you, where there's smoke, there's fire."

"Wait a minute. Why do you think it was Ruth?"

"I got a Christmas card this year from her with a note that said, 'Ben was so good to me. He was a good friend.' Why did she need to say that? When I read it, I remembered that old letter, and suddenly I put two and two together." Her eyes filled with tears. "What a damn fool I was."

I don't want to believe this. "Didn't she have a husband?"

"She did. He worked nights."

"Doing what?"

"Painting prisons."

"Mom, are you sure? I never heard of a job like that."

"It's true. She left her last job because she was having an affair with the owner of the bar. That's how Daddy hired her."

"Then she repeated it?"

My mother nods. "He always said a penis has no morals."

Never ever before in all the years of my life did my mother infer that my father had genitals. And now they are even going in the wrong place? All along it was right in front of her—someone even notified her—but now she is facing up to it?

Wasn't this true with Roshi too, when I pictured him and Eleanor in the zendo together? It was right there. And my father's abuse with me? No one wanted to see it. Anyone who looked could have known.

My mother gazes across the room at me. Her black eyes are glowing. Her mouth is determined, lips pressed together. She opens and then clenches her hands on the two arms of the old TV chair that used to be my father's. A gold band is still on her left third finger.

I feel nauseous. I get up to open a window. I can hardly breathe.

"Don't do that. The rain'll come in."

A burst of thunder cracks in the distance. I jump and slam the window shut.

"You met her once. You were a little girl."

I fumble with the venetian blind. "I don't remember." She is not going to change this subject.

"Do you have a phone number?" I ask. I should get to the bottom of this—who am I kidding? We have already gotten there. We are right at the rudiment, the bone, the core.

Was this what made her so unhappy in my childhood? Why she was always preoccupied and ignored her young daughter?

The roles have been switched. The rug has once again been pulled out from under me. My mother wants to get to the truth that underscored her life.

I sit down on the edge of the couch. I can't stay still. I jump up again. "I'm going to the pool."

Her mouth falls open. "In the rain? At night? Are you crazy? You'll get electrocuted."

"I'll take a shower." I run into the bathroom before she can say another word.

I've had a disdain for Tuesdays all my life and never could figure out why. I had no aversion for any other day of the week. I thought it was some personal idiosyncrasy. In my thirties I wrote a poem that began, "A girl sometimes wonders / if her father slept around." I took a leap into what I thought was my imagination for the next stanza, "My father did / I didn't want to believe it / but my father did sleep around."

I didn't mention Tuesday in that poem. But standing

naked in the brown-tiled shower my father and mother stood up in a thousand times before, I know that that second workday of the week, the one I pictured as a sickening yellow, should have been in my verse. When I'd read that poem publicly, the room of people always moved into a deep apprehensive silence, the way they did when I recited the one about my father and World War II. Was there a connection? How many daughters had fathers who had extramarital affairs while they were growing up?

I reach for the hot knob and turn it off, stand in the blazing cold water that no human ever gets used to, and let it penetrate me.

TE-SHAN'S DISCIPLE Yen-t'ou eventually became Te-shan's lineage holder and an extraordinary teacher with many students. This was at the end of the Tang dynasty, when there was much disruption in the land. Bandits roamed freely everywhere. The frightened monks left the monastery and hid in the surrounding forest. Only Yen-t'ou remained at the temple, where he continued to meditate.

One day the head bandit stalked through the temple grounds. Enraged that there were no treasures, he pulled out his sword. In front of him sat Yen-t'ou totally composed. The thief ran the blade through the great Zen adept.

Yen-t'ou let out a scream that was heard in the woods for thirty miles around. And then he died.

Was he scared, angry, horrified? What are we to make of that yell? A shout that resounded that far a distance had to plumb the depths. It was the total expression of his life. Whatever was there he encountered it. He did not turn away. This time what he came upon was his death. He faced it completely.

Much later he was given the name "Clear Severity."

I GRAB THE YELLOW TOWEL from the hook behind the door. How old would Ruth be now? Late sixties?

I bend over to wipe my feet, run the cloth over my calves.

I see the Aero Tavern in my mind's eye, the place my father worked for thirty years in the town where I was brought up. My father is handing a glass of whiskey to Harry, an old regular who sways over to the bathroom. Ruth is drying down the counter. The distributor rolls in a keg through the front door, the Rheingold light flashes, and the phone is ringing. Above it hangs a round plaster print of my hand that I made for my father in kindergarten. My mother is calling to tell her husband to pick up a quart of milk and a loaf of bread for dinner on the way home. But now I see something else too: a trapdoor on the ceiling. I remember my father mentioning it once, another way out, in case there was trouble. The Mafia, the cops, you never know. Could my father and Ruth, half-dressed, have climbed out?

I stand up and shake out my wet head. There never is another way out. Only the straight way. My mother has revealed herself to me.

I take a deep breath. I throw on one of her night-gowns and march right back into the living room.

I fold my arms around her, leaning over the chair.

My mother looks up and says, "I love you," touches my elbow.

My heart is pounding. I almost hesitate. I say it back. And I mean it. I actually truly mean it.

Epilogue

L AST SUMMER I WENT to the races at Saratoga Springs.
I bet to win, place, and show on Old Crow in the first
round. The horse had six-to-one odds. Better than Midnight Summit at thirty to one. My father would have
approved of the probabilities. But he wouldn't have liked
how I chose. I ran my finger down the names and picked
the one that had juice for me, contained glitter, held a
possibility.

I'd learned this from writing. What topics, however
illogically, called out? An onion? A poppy-seed roll?
Upstate New York, where my father first learned to bet?
What would unwind the story inside?

My father also wouldn't have liked that I put down six
dollars on three positions. "You pick one and go with it."

I screamed bloody murder when my number pulled
out from the middle near the last stretch and streamed
past the lead horse. I yelled so loud and so shrill, it was
surprising the horses didn't halt right in front of me. I
didn't care about the elegance or beauty, or how the jockeys seemed to be holding themselves stationary above the

saddles in spite of the pounding flesh and bones beneath. I only cared about the power: the three tickets in my hot little hand, my own great victory. I'd made it to this place and was winning.

Carol, who'd come with me, said, never ever, even at a Bob Dylan concert, had she heard me so loud.

Really I was calling my father back into triumph this early August afternoon in the crowded bleachers, as I looked at the battered turf. Each year it gets harder. The truth of his never returning, beaten deeper into me. The fourth year had come and gone. This person I loved is not coming back.

The man behind the counter punched in my wins, and the computer popped up fourteen dollars.

"Only fourteen?" I asked. This was no way to make a living.

I stuffed the bills into my pants pocket.

The next day I walked the town's streets and tried to imagine what it was like for my father at eighteen, the first time he'd left home by himself with all his savings for a cross-country trip. He never got beyond Saratoga and the track. He lost every penny over a few days. He didn't care. He had a great time, returning to Brooklyn with the discovery of a whole new sport and a new thing to do.

In a side alley I found an antique shop with old jewelry. I went in and pointed to a large ring in the showcase.

"These were big in the twenties and thirties. It has the same structure as a ruby, only it's synthetic." The clerk was bald with thick eyebrows.

I had one of those rings at home in a small black velvet box—my inheritance. I'd never seen another before. I left the store and felt my father all over the place. This was his world.

I stood on the corner curb. You live and then you die, I thought. It's good to have some good times. My father certainly did that. When people used to say to him, you have such a talented daughter, he'd reply, "My wife and I are ordinary. She did this all on her own."

I don't wonder much what he would have thought about this writing.

"You got it all wrong," he might have said. "You always were a rotten kid. You thought too much." He'd pause. "Make sure to tell them I loved your mother, how beautiful my eyes were, how good my girls were—yeah, you and the little one." He'd stop again. "And, Nat, I'm proud of you. I don't understand what you do, but you've got a heck of a lot of nerve."

When my father first opened the tavern, two beefy men marched in, and behind them three movers plunked down along the north wall a jukebox and a cigarette machine.

"You pay us. We collect once a week." They turned and left.

My father served fourteen drinks in the next hour, eight of which were tap ale. Four football players from the nearby agricultural college were standing at the bar.

"Fellas, help push these out."

He left the equipment on the street. Word got around, and the Mafia arrived within the hour.

"I didn't order anything from you." My father stared them down.

"I got dumb lucky. They left and never bothered me again."

Any nerve I got I inherited from him.

AND THEN I WONDER WHAT ROSHI, dead now thirteen years, would have thought. I've even stopped waiting for his return. Could he ever have existed? It feels as though he's taken his place as a distant star. I won't say this too loudly, because I don't want my adored father to hear, but Katagiri Roshi was the most important human being in my life.

After I die and my ashes are sprinkled in the places I love—the Jewish cemetery in Taos, the artists' cemetery in Woodstock, by the Mississippi near New Albin, Iowa, with my blood family on Long Island—I wouldn't want people to say of me only "She was a great teacher" or "I loved her writing." I would like at least one person to come closer, to add, "She was also lonely, she suffered a lot. She was mixed up. She made some big mistakes." Then tell those mistakes and sum up: "But she was important to me." Then I would feel really honored, as though someone had seen and known me.

Roshi was a private man. He came from a private culture. It is American to march out our feelings, the particulars of our life, to meet someone at a party, pat them on the back, tell them all our stories.

Roshi knew my deep history, beyond where I was born, who my parents were, my favorite food, what colors I liked. In every human existence, we are telling the history of a people. Roshi reached beyond the details to show me the patterns of suffering and pointed out the path to freedom. But it wasn't holy or abstract. We sat across from each other, and he knew me—the stinky Natalie, as he would say, and the great one.

I'm not sure he would have thanked me for what I have written. A long time ago he had thanked me for my effort. Once for four years I pursued Gary Snyder to come to Minnesota and do a benefit for Zen Center. When Snyder finally arrived, I was in Israel on a poetry fellowship. But three months later when I returned, Roshi acknowledged me. It was a simple thing. I was sitting across the table from him the first time back at the center.

"Gary Snyder was here." He nodded. "Thank you." There was a long pause—time enough for me to feel his appreciation.

In those days I felt the power of silence. Since then I have also understood something else: that silence protects no one. I have heard it often repeated: keep it in the family. That only continues the suffering.

But Roshi deserves the same treatment he gave to me. I can also look beyond "stinky Katagiri." With his own great effort, he planted the seed of an enormous gift into the soil of this country. And he did it person to person. I could have read a book about Buddhism, Zen, meditation. Instead, he practiced with me moment by moment. He taught me the most simple, democratic thing—how to sit still in the center of this busy world. You need no fancy equipment, no special intelligence or talent. This one thing turned my whole life—affected how I write, eat, walk, think, and don't think. It has rooted inside me, so that after everything else has been said, every story told, I will never forget it. Even after my ashes are spread, something will abound with an endless gratitude.